# PRAISE FOR FAUST RUGGIERO AND
## *THE FIX YOUSELF HANDBOOK*

*SILVER WINNER,*
*Nonfiction Authors Association Book Awards*

"*The Fix Yourself Handbook* offers an interesting range of approaches to becoming more objective and less emotional about life experiences in order to stay centered and peaceful. The formulas suggested can clearly be helpful for people who are working with counselors in therapy or recovery programs and also for readers seeking guidance to create more self-discipline."

—NONFICTION AUTHORS ASSOCIATION BOOK AWARDS

"*The Fix Yourself Handbook* is an action-filled plan for decreasing negativity, increasing joy, and embracing yourself. It presents a clear direction for an improved and enhanced life.

—JENNIFER NOLL FOR INDIEREADER BOOK REVIEWS

"Faust Ruggiero has devised a unique psychological method by which anyone might find a better direction for coping with life's challenges."

—BARBARA BAMBERGER SCOTT, US REVIEW

"The chapters are very well-structured; they follow a pattern that makes a wealth of information easy to understand and navigate. I felt that this is an actual handbook that readers can use as a reference, going back t⟩ _____ _____ challenges in life."

⟩NLINEBOOKCLUB.ORG

D1281807

# THE
# FIX YOURSELF
# HANDBOOK

## Using the Process Way of Life to Transform Your Life into a Happy, Healthy Journey

## FAUST RUGGIERO, M.S.

FYHB PUBLISHING

*Published by:*
**FYHB Publishing**
BANGOR, PA
www.faustruggiero.com

ISBNs:
Paperback: 978-1-7343830-0-3
Ebook: 978-1-7343830-1-0

Cover and interior design by Gary A. Rosenberg
www.thebookcouple.com

Printed in the United States of America

# Contents

*No one can fix your world for you.*
*Everything you need to be happy and*
*fulfilled is already inside you.*
*You simply need to understand how to use it.*
*Then you can find peace,*
*and begin to love yourself.*

# *The Fix Yourself Handbook—*
## From the Office to the Bookshelf

MY PROFESSIONAL CAREER SPANS OVER FORTY YEARS. I have counseled clients ranging in age from five, and into senior living. I have counseled people in inpatient facilities, prisons, substance abuse counseling centers, in nursing homes, provided employee assistance programs to major corporations, and have extensive experience providing emotional support services to deaf children. I was part of a team that developed the counseling program for drunk drivers that became the prototype for the state of Pennsylvania, and is still being used in many other states. I continue to provide counseling services for veterans, first responders, law enforcement, and other emergency personnel. I have taught at the college level, and am published in several research journals.

I've been in private practice at the Community Psychological Center, in Bangor, Pennsylvania for over thirty years, specializing in individual, family, substance abuse, women's issues, and marital/couples counseling. During that time, I developed the Process Way of Life, and have used it with over 2,000 of my clients, helping them to realize and unleash the power they have inside themselves. With the Process Way of Life being so successful as a counseling program, I decided to develop the process-based journey into a written text. The approach underwent several years of research and program design, so that it could effectively be communicated in written form. I want all of you to understand how to present your problems, to understand them, and I want to provide you with the exact steps to fix those problems. The Process Way of Life has now been developed into a written version of the original counseling program, and is presented here in *The Fix Yourself Handbook*.

I have been featured on television, radio, in newspaper columns, and continue to counsel, and conduct workshops and trainings about the Process Way of Life. For more information, please visit my website at www.faustruggiero.com.

◇◇◇◇◇◇◇◇◇◇◇◇◇◇◇◇◇◇

# The Master Plan

WHO AMONG US HASN'T SEARCHED FOR A WAY to understand ourselves, alleviate negativity, and learn to like and eventually love who we are? *The Fix Yourself Handbook's* Process Way of Life helps you gain a better understanding of how you think, feel, and behave, and how important becoming *internally balanced* is to your personal growth, and to your happiness. You can fix any problem you have when you understand that *you already have everything you need inside you* to live a happy and healthy life. You simply need to learn how to access your powers.

Human beings are a product of nature. As such, we are governed by natural rules. These are called *processes*: deliberate and natural actions or steps that must be performed so that we can live in tune with our own natural flow. Understanding the processes, which are listed and defined later in this introduction, and learning how to incorporate them into your life, will help you understand yourself better, and help you live a more happy and productive life.

## THE PROCESS WAY OF LIFE

The Process Way of Life presented in this book is a step-by-step program that can transform your life into one that is happy, healthy, purposeful, and content. Who we are is the product of the interplay between our physical, intellectual, emotional, and spiritual attributes; which we all have. Understanding and learning to live according to the Process Way of Life will eventually lead to the ultimate goal of the program: internal balance. You will achieve internal balance when these four attributes operate together, providing you with a pure loving energy source that will change your life. Learning to love yourself, and to apply your love to others is the enduring final gift of the Process Way of Life.

*The Fix Yourself Handbook* presents the Process Way of Life as a journey that begins as you decide that your life is not as happy and productive as you would like it to be. Everything starts when you decide to become an active player in your life; when you are willing to begin the journey to transform your anger to love, and your sadness to joy, so that you may create your own happy and productive life.

The journey begins with the first four of its fifty-two unique processes (presented in nineteen separate categories) for living; the Process Way of Living's opening process bookends. They are Fact-Finding (part of the Present/Understand/Fix formula (Chapter 2), Brutal Honesty (Chapter 3), Intellect Over Emotion (Chapter 4), and Slowing Down Life's Pace (Chapter 5). They set the stage for the transforming life journey that will teach you about yourself, help you to learn to like yourself, and eventually to love yourself.

These chapters are followed by twenty-four information- and advice-filled chapters that support the Process Way of Life journey, and teach you what you need to be healthy and happy. The second set of process bookends, Gratitude (Chapter 30), In-service Chapter 31), and Faith (Chapter 32) initiate the closing stages of the journey, bringing you to internal balance, and finally pure love. The book closes with The Journey Within (the book's summary chapter), and Good Housekeeping: The Never-Ending Process Gift, which provides you with the process you will use to protect the changes you are making.

Each bite-sized chapter targets a specific human issue. The causes of your problems and how they exert their influence over you are discussed, and the precise steps to help you correct the problem are provided as the chapter winds down. I've designed this program so you may apply the steps to your own life circumstances, as they exist in *your* life. However, as you will see, the problems presented here are experienced by all of us at one time or another. You are not as different as you think you are, and there is a logical way out of your distress.

The Process Way of Life is the product of over twenty years of practical counseling application. With an expertise on both research and counseling, I have developed the program, researched it extensively, and have used it with my clients for over two decades. It's a dynamic addition to an existing counseling program, or for those of you who may have difficulty obtaining professional counseling, it can provide you with either a viable alternative, or an introduction to that step.

The book will provide you with the tools to change your life initially, and will always be available as a reference guide, and a lifelong support ally. If you are willing to give the Process Way of Life time to grow, it will become an invaluable part of everything you choose to do.

You are greater than the problems you think define your life. In fact, you are great. So, get ready to become the master of your destiny. Prepare yourself for the most exciting journey of your life!

## HOW TO USE THE BOOK

Each chapter title in the book introduces the information that will be covered in the chapter. A short slogan follows the title, highlighting the chapter's overall message. Beneath the slogan, you'll find the "Processes to Employ," which lists the specific processes you will be using to address the problem being explored in that chapter. You can refer back to the definition of the processes in the introduction to refresh yourself when you need to. The body of each chapter provides all the information to help you understand the problem being presented. You will see helpful steps throughout the chapters in the text being presented in groups of seven. I did this to help make it easier for you to remember and for you to apply them.

So, to start the chapter, I'll *present* the problem. The discussion that follows will help you *understand* it, and at the end of each chapter, you will find the section "Time To Take Action," which provides the action steps you can take to help you *fix* that problem. I will be using an approach I call the Present/Understand/Fix formula throughout the book. This will be discussed in more detail in Chapter 2. Each chapter closes with a "declaration" to help you move forward with the theme of the chapter, and a short "Onward" piece that introduces the next chapter. Every chapter in the book follows this format, making it easier for you to navigate through, and apply the information.

Read each chapter slowly. In each chapter, you will learn how to apply specific processes to help you address the concerns presented in that chapter. Think of the processes as tools you can use to help you change your world, and trust that they have the potential to help you find happiness. Take your time as you read the detailed explanation of each problem so that you may understand why that problem exists. Then, follow the advice provided in the steps at the end of the chapter.

Go slow. You may even want to read the chapters twice. The chapters are short, but there is an abundance of information contained in each. Move on only when you are sure that you understood what you have read, and how to apply the advice given at the end of the chapter. I advise that you read only one chapter per day. This will give you some time to think about what you're reading, understand it, and begin to apply the advice chapter provides.

When you're done with the book, think about reading it again. You're going to find that after a second time through, you will understand the information better, and you will be more proficient at applying the advice the book provides. Remember, it's a program for life, so don't worry about how good you are at applying the advice now. You're going to continue to get better. If you remain committed, good things are going to happen for you.

*The Fix Yourself Handbook's* Process Way of Life is written as a journey. It, however, being a life journey, does not come to a conclusion when you are finished with the book. The Process Way of Life has been designed to be with you all of your life, and your growth will continue each day of your life, for the rest of your life. I wrote the book as a journey to simulate life's journey, and what will happen as your life continues to unfold. So, think of the book as a micro-journey, a small representation of what will happen if you continue to make the Process Way of Life the way you live your own life.

Notes: As you read through *The Fix Yourself Handbook*, you will notice that the text is geared for people who need to slow down life's pace. In today's culture, that tends to apply to the majority of people. For some, especially where depression is involved, slowing down may not apply. For those of you who are having a difficult time motivating yourself, or who experience periods of lethargy or lack of direction, it makes good sense to visit a physician to determine if anything may be affecting you on a physical level. Start there first.

Also, throughout the book, you will see that in many of the chapters, I am suggesting that you either talk about a problem with someone you trust, or with a professional counselor. No one navigates through life's roadblocks alone all the time. From time-to-time, you might need a little help. Though you may feel that you don't need anyone else's assistance, be willing to obtain that help as a support to the advice you are receiving from me, if necessary. Life is about options, and having others to support you through the tough times is, at times, one of those options.

## THE PROCESS WAY OF LIFE "BOOKENDS"

While there are fifty-two processes I'll be covering in this book, four of these processes are the cornerstones of the Process Way of Life program. As I mentioned above, these four processes set the stage for the work you will be doing, and little will change in your life if you don't use them properly. They are:

1. Fact-Finding (part of the Present/Understand/Fix formula (Chapter 2)

2. Brutal Honesty (Chapter 3)

**3.** I Over E, or Intellect Over Emotion (Chapter 4)

**4.** Slowing Down Life's Pace (Chapter 5)

You will need these processes to work the entire program. They will be presented as "Processes to Employ" in every chapter in the book. Near the end of the book, you will find the second set of process bookends. They are:

**1.** Gratitude (Chapter 30)

**2.** In-service (Chapter 31)

**3.** Faith (Chapter 32)

When you understand how to apply these three processes, you have come to that part of the Process Way of Life that will provide you with a deeper understanding of internal balance—that state when all of your internal attributes function in equilibrium. When this happens, pure love, the most important power source that the Process Way of Life provides, can be realized.

The Process Way of Life is your guide on an exciting and enlightening life journey that will touch every part of you. Let the processes take you there. The Process Way of Life creates one of life's most exciting and wondrous life journeys, and yours is about to begin.

# THE PROCESSES—
# CATEGORIES AND DESCRIPTIONS

| | Process | Description |
|---|---|---|
| 1 | **Personal Inventory** (Alternate and/or related terms: *Internal Focus, Morality*) | The process of focusing our energy inward to allow for the identification of personal strengths and self-understanding, with the goal of understanding our personal principles concerning the distinction between right and wrong. |
| 2 | **Slow and Steady** (Alternate and/or related terms: *Patience, Slowing Down Life's Pace, Incremental Forward Movement*) | The movement away from quick and impulsive behaviors, and into a state of willful tolerance of delay through the deceleration of a lifestyle that leads to poor decisions and internal conflict, with the understanding that only through small, well-planned steps can we create sustained change and improve the quality of our lives. |
| 3 | **Honesty** (Alternate and/or related terms: *Brutal Honesty, Humility, Truth-Telling*) | The process of being absolutely honest with ourselves, even to the point of personal discomfort, and choosing to take a modest view of our own importance for the purposes of opening oneself up to personal growth. |
| 4 | **I Over E (Intellect over Emotion)** (Alternate and/or related terms: *Emotional Control, Fact-Finding, Intelligent Decision-Making*) | Taking the steps necessary to reduce the impact of emotions on our intellectual processes, and using our intellect to exhaustively search for the facts in situations that may lead to stress and personal problems, before our emotions have an opportunity to distort them. Cultivating the understanding that knowledge must be applied so it may become a parameter of personal growth. |
| 5 | **Present/Understand/ Fix** (Alternate and/or related terms: *Fact-Finding*) | The formula you will use in every chapter to address your problems. You present the problem, you use the facts to understand it, and you take the steps to fix it. |

| 6 | **Surrendering to the Process** (Alternate and/or related terms: *Trust, Faith, Belief, Honor, Dignity*) | The willingness to have unconditional trust, either in a process or some unknown entity, such as a higher power, and to allow ourselves to become subservient to the processes, so that we can learn to believe in ourselves, knowing we are capable of being the person we want to be. Having learned to do this, we can learn to think, feel, and behave in a fashion that raises our consciousness to higher-order thoughts and feelings, and connects us to our innermost spirit. |
| --- | --- | --- |
| 7 | **Effective Communication** (Alternate and/or related terms: *Warm Confrontation, Positive Language Reciprocity, Communication, Conflict Resolution, Listening*) | Understanding and mastering the art of positive information exchanges. The ability to gather the facts, understand them, place them in an internally cohesive framework, and present that framework, intelligently, to others to address problems. Learning to listen to ourselves, and to others, even if the information presents challenges. Understanding that the way we speak to ourselves and others can set the stage for how we feel about ourselves, and how we communicate with others. |
| 8 | **Cleaning House** (Alternate and/or related terms: *Life Inventory, Eliminating Toxic People, Housekeeping, Gatekeeping, Boundary-Setting*) | The honest review of one's life, and those relationships in it. The removal of all people, events, and situations that may cause pain, conflict, confusion, or dysfunction from one's life to make way for positive and functional information and life-enhancing processes, followed by the practice of monitoring who and what may enter our lives thereafter. Setting boundaries regarding who gets in, and how close, and learning to defend those boundaries. |
| 9 | **Simplifying Life** (Alternate and/or related terms: *Life on Life's Terms, Keeping Life Simple, Life's Natural Flow*) | Understanding how to apply life's natural flow in our lives, along with the removal of any irrational, unreasonable expectations, and unnecessary complexity from life to make room for a simpler and more productive way of living. |

| 10 | **Living the Journey** (Alternate and/ or related terms: *Reduction of Destination Living, One-Day-at-a-Time Living, Living in the Moment, Journey Living, Creativity, Passion, Humor*) | Releasing one's attachment to a happiness in life that is dependent on one's arrival at specific, magnificent destinations in favor of focusing on the present, with minimum movement back to past people and events, or forward to events which have not yet occurred. The willingness to focus all life energy on our present life and happiness, moment by moment, as life is being lived, and to appreciate the lighter sides of life, thus reducing stress and pain. |
|---|---|---|
| 11 | **Closure on the Past** (Alternate and/or related terms: *Settling Past Issues, Forgiveness*) | Judiciously reviewing all past situations and events to put closure on them. Once we've done this, we undertake a step-by-step process to understand what we and others have done wrong, to make amends, and allow ourselves to move forward with reduced emotional pain; forgiving ourselves, and others who may have hurt us. |
| 12 | **Eyes on the Prize** (Alternate and/or related terms: *Goal-Setting, Time/Energy Management, Learning to Be Comfortable with Being Uncomfortable, Risk-Taking*) | The practice of setting a long-term goal, complete with short-term goals, action steps, and an executable plan to carry them out in a coherent, cohesive, and timely fashion, and then consciously managing our daily clock and applying our energy to healthy modes of thought and behavior. Accepting that temporary, uncomfortable time frames lead to the happiness and the fulfillment we seek, and that change, by definition, is unsettling, but it is where understanding and growth live. |
| 13 | **Commitment** | Enduring dedication; the Process Way of Life takes time, and continuous, unwavering commitment to the program is essential to ensure its success. |
| 14 | **Service** (Alternate and/or related terms: *Being in Service*) | The willingness to turn our rewards outward to help serve the needs of others without expectation of notoriety or payback. |

| 15 | **Wisdom** (Alternate and/ or related terms: *Sustained Learning, Humility*) | Being committed to remaining an eternal student of life's lessons and positive teaching sources so we can reach our goal of having the experience, knowledge, and good judgment to achieve an understanding of the bigger picture in life, and how to apply ourselves there. |
|---|---|---|
| 16 | **Gratitude** | The understanding that we must be grateful for all we are, all we have, and all we can be, and that we must express this in every moment of our lives. |
| 17 | **Maintaining the Program** (Alternate and/ or related terms: *System Maintenance, Housekeeping*) | The establishment and maintenance of an internally balanced power source where the intellect, emotions, body, and spirit become one. This power source is always alive and functional, emanating from inside ourselves. |
| 18 | **Internal Balance** | This is the goal of the program. It is the point where our physical, intellectual, emotional, and spiritual attributes operate in a state of enhanced equilibrium. |
| 19 | **Pure Love** | That point in the Process Way of Life where, through internal balance, we allow our new power source to be realized, to wrap itself around all we feel, touch, see, and do. This is love at its purest level. |

◇◇◇◇◇◇◇◇◇◇◇◇

# CHAPTER 1

# Disengaging Life's Unhealthy Routines

## TAKING LIFE OFF AUTOPILOT

*Only you can change the person you are. Make your first decision to become an active player in your own life. Take your life off autopilot.*

---

**PROCESSES TO EMPLOY:** Brutal Honesty, I Over E, Present/ Understand/Fix, Slowing Down Life's Pace, Internal Focus

---

MAKING THE RIGHT CHOICES CAN ENHANCE the quality of your life. Change pulls you out of your safe place, that divine comfort zone we all love, and out of your customary routine. Life seems much easier when you don't have to make difficult decisions, and when you're not challenged by circumstances which are either foreign to you, or cause you to exert more effort than you would like. Deciding to be an active decision-maker can run counter to that spontaneous and uncomplicated lifestyle so many of us enjoy.

## What Is Life on Autopilot?

The typical human mode of operation is to run our lives in accordance with our established routines. We like our lives to be effortless and comfortable, with little applied thought. We want things to be easy, and unchallenging. The unfortunate consequence of living life this way is that our brains never really learn to become efficient at making important life decisions. It's not unlike what happens when an airplane pilot puts his navigation system on autopilot. By doing this, he minimizes the amount of interaction between his brain and the airplane's technology.

I'm defining "living on autopilot" as *the tendency to minimize your brain's interaction with its environment regarding the choices you make, and the way you carry out your daily life.* Living like this, though it may keep you feeling comfortable, seriously limits your ability to make decisions, because you are simply not receiving enough new information. You will need this information to create the options that will help you make the changes in your life that are important to you. This is where you make the decision to become that active player in your own life. It's time to take your life off autopilot.

## The Risk of Crashing

When your brain becomes lulled into autopilot living, you can allow yourself to remain in situations that range from numb to toxic. The reduction in the quality of your life, something that should irritate and frustrate you, doesn't seem to bother you anymore. As this condition progresses, you adjust to this uninspired way of living, and stop questioning it. As this intellectual paralysis progresses, you become increasingly adept at living both uninspired, and unmotivated.

Since your brain is no longer efficiently analyzing information, people, places, things, and situations that are damaging you become a normal way of living life. Soon enough, you become as toxic as the conditions that initially poisoned you. Call this insanity by association. If you allow your brain to sleep its way through your life, it is no longer making enough of the important decisions for you. As a result, you will allow others to do so, and you will follow the crowd to places that can eventually injure you, and make you very unhappy.

This autopilot way of living life is wrought with growth-inhibiting boundaries, and intellectual and emotional limitations. Small challenges become monumental, and you may compromise your ability to formulate the plans you need to grow and achieve your goals. You may lose your passion for growth, often setting no long-term goals. You can stop dreaming, and soon, you begin regretting the course your life is taking.

Autopilot is a predetermined life setting, whose only purpose is to take you from one preset point to the next. Unfortunately, growth does not occur at the beginning or end of a destination. It's the choices and experiences between those two life points that help you grow. By limiting the acquisition of important information, autopilot living removes most of the choices you should be making between destinations. It's a preprogrammed, robotic way to live life. Here's an example:

> Robert is a middle-aged father of two, and works as a personnel manager in an office close to his home. Each morning, he leaves the house, goes to his office, sits in that office, does his work, and returns home at the end of his day. When he arrives home, he spends a little time in his workshop, eats supper, and then watches television for the remainder of the evening. On weekends, he again spends time in his workshop, in front of the television, and may go out to eat with his wife. Robert seems happy, but as you can see, his life is routine, mundane, and offers little room for growth. There are no challenges in Robert's life. He is in an autopilot rut.

Think about how much different Robert's life would be if he took his mind off of autopilot, began to examine some of the choices that are available to him, and started making a few simple changes in the way he is living. More choices could lead to a deeper sense of satisfaction in his life, and he might experience some personal growth from his new lifestyle.

# Taking Hold of the Reins

Human beings, by definition, were created to evolve and grow. You live in a world of constant forward progression. Nothing stands still, and everything around you is ever-changing. To assume that you can live your life by reducing your connection to a dynamic forward-moving world is foolhardy. You must learn to examine the information in any situation, make healthy decisions, and take control of your life to meet the constantly changing needs of an evolving world.

In the truest sense, you are a decision-maker; the master of your own destiny. You must steadfastly prepare yourself for forward movement, always monitoring the world around you. You must make decisions that help you to meet the needs of a progressive and compelling human experience that is always changing. You must take control of your life, and understand that there is no place for autopilot living. To live and function in a world that never stops changing, you must move away from the stagnation that life on autopilot creates, and become your own dynamic decision-maker.

The ability to make conscious choices, regardless of how small they are, stimulates the brain, creates new experiences, promotes learning, induces a passion for growth, and helps keep you away from toxic people and situations. To move forward with the Process Way of Life, it is imperative that you are willing to disconnect the automatic pilot from your life, stop following the crowd, and be willing to make some of those decisions you have been avoiding. If you think you're running your life on autopilot, this is how you begin to reverse the process.

##  Time To Take Action

1. Start by making small decisions and choices rather than important life-defining decisions. Take the minor situations in your life, simple things that you routinely do each day, like your daily schedule, and what you do in your personal time, and make subtle changes in them.

2. Eliminate some of your repetitive behaviors, and replace them with some activities you typically don't do. The simple changes will activate your brain, and help you interact with your environment, as it pulls you out of your autopilot rut.

3. Challenge your daily routines. Do things a bit differently. Change the sequence, the duration, and the content of even the simple things that you do every day. Now, include a few new pursuits that make you think about what you need to do. This infuses your day with conscious thought, instead of autopilot robotry.

4. Don't just go through the motions. Try to think about everything you are doing. Put more conscious thought in your entire day. Think, then do.

## Driving It Home

I'm going to be presenting a great deal of information as we move forward in the Process Way of Life, and you're going to be making many changes. Your first change is to take your brain off autopilot as you begin to review information, and make more conscious decisions. This is precisely where decision-making comes into play. Learn to experience your life as an active player in it. An engaged brain understands how to make intelligent decisions. You do have choices, so get your brain back in the game.

**YOUR DECLARATION IS:** *I will disengage, so I can engage.*

### 🚶 ONWARD

With your autopilot life-chaperone securely disengaged, it's time to turn your attention to the formula that will help you understand and employ these processes that comprise the Process Way of Life. It's time to learn how to present it, understand it, and fix it.

# CHAPTER 2

# A Practical Formula to Fix Your Life

## PRESENT/UNDERSTAND/FIX

*Stop obsessing! Present the problem honestly. Understand everything about it. Then, fix the problem. It's that simple.*

**PROCESSES TO EMPLOY:** Brutal Honesty, I Over E, Present/ Understand/Fix, Slowing Down Life's Pace, Fact Finding

FOR ALMOST EVERY PROBLEM WE ENCOUNTER IN LIFE, there is a solution. As you proceed with the Process Way of Life, you'll be using a targeted approach to help you address your concerns. In the chapters that comprise the book, keep a close watch on how the issues are *presented*, how relevant information is gathered, providing an enhanced *understanding* of the problems, which leads to action-able solutions to address and *fix* them. Let's explore the approach in detail.

## The Formula for Success

The procedure you are going to be using is Present/Understand/Fix. This procedure will set the stage for everything you will do moving forward in the Process Way of Life. It is, in its truest form, a formula for healthy problem solving, and ultimately, healthy living. Regardless of how happy you feel, from time to time, you will encounter difficult people and situations. It's important to be able to define the problem, understand the facts associated with the issue, and formulate and carry out the steps to fix the problem. Doing so leads to positive life choices. The present/understand/fix formula does just that.

### Present/Understand/Fix: Explained

1. The presentation stage is simply the initial introduction of the problem. Here, you want to state what happened (or is happening) as straightforwardly as you possibly can. Helpful hint: The only facts you are looking for in the presentation stage are clear, concise statements about what is concerning you. Present the problem; that's all.

2. Having stated your initial concern, you can begin the second stage of the formula. In the understanding stage, you want to collect the facts. Your objective is to gather as much of the supportive information as you can to provide the big-picture view you will need to help you formulate a plan to fix your problem. This will include all the people, places, and events associated with your problem. Helpful hint: Do your best to keep your emotions out of the process. You want just the facts now.

As you will learn in Chapter 4, your emotions can lead to misrepresentation of facts, and you want to avoid that. Your ability to solve your problem will always relate directly to the accuracy of your information. In the understanding stage, stay close to the facts, present them as they have occurred, and keep any personal agendas out of the picture. Once you have the facts, it's all right to express how you feel about what has happened.

3. You now have the information you need to devise and execute a plan to enter the final stage of the formula: to *fix the problem*. Now, you can use all of that information, some of which will also include your feelings about the problem, and devise a solution that can efficiently address your concerns. Helpful hint:

Information presented factually will always point you in the direction of a viable solution. As you will learn in Chapter 3, *honesty*, coupled with *factual information* (which proceeds emotional infusion), provides you with the best opportunity to succeed. You present, you understand, you fix. I will be using this approach in every chapter in the book.

##  TIME TO TAKE ACTION

1. Regardless of what happens in your life, try to keep your emotions out of it. Present the events exactly as they have occurred. If you need to, talk it over with another (unbiased) person. I'm going to address using your intellect over your emotion, and working with factual information in detail in Chapter 4.

2. You need information. Following an accurate presentation of your problem, get as much information as you can about the problem. Be honest and clear about the information. You only want the facts now.

3. Ask yourself where your emotions are at this point. If you think your emotions may be altering the facts just a bit, sit down with someone you trust. Review the information. Let them ask you questions to help you put things in perspective.

4. Now that you have the facts, you'll be able to see the picture more clearly. Follow these steps to begin to fix your problem:

   A. Since you have the information, it makes sense to compile a list of what you may need to do to address your problem.

   B. Prioritize your list. This will tell you which information should be addressed first.

   C. Begin with your most important item first, and work your way down the list. Doing so usually brings you to your solution.

 **DRIVING IT HOME**

From this point on, everything you do throughout the Process Way of Life program will follow the Present/Understand/Fix formula. You will see the problem presented in the first paragraph. The body of the chapter will provide the information you need, and the action steps at the end of the chapter will tell you how to fix the problem. It's a simple model for a formula you can use to address your entire life.

**YOUR DECLARATION IS**: *I will Present it, I will Understand it, I will Fix it.*

 **ONWARD**

Most of us firmly believe we are honest. We're going to learn how to take honesty to an entirely new level; one that will help you find and understand the person you really are. Welcome to Brutal Honesty!

# CHAPTER 3

# Brutal Honesty: The Real Test of Courage

*Take an honest look inside yourself. There is someone special locked up in there; someone who doesn't need all the lies and games.*
*Let them out.*

**PROCESSES TO EMPLOY:** Brutal Honesty, I Over E, Present/ Understand/Fix, Slowing Down Life's Pace, Fact-Finding, Truth-Telling

HONESTY IS THAT SO SACRED VIRTUE THAT so many of us firmly believe defines who we are. We all say we want to be treated honestly by other people. The problem with honesty, and with our ability to accept honesty from other people, is that it can so drastically differ from that version of the healthy and sensible person we may firmly believe we are. All too often, it's our version of the facts that we want to hear.

## The Truth Hurts

We all like to think we are strong, well-balanced people who have a good grasp on who we are, what we think, and how we feel. We can take great offense to any form of criticism from others, and have a difficult time understanding what to do when someone provides us with information that runs counter to our own beliefs.

The truth of the matter is, most of us really don't want any part of real honesty. Honesty has evolved into a concept that has less to do with factual information, and more to do with emotional survival. We will do whatever it takes to protect our fragile and spurious feelings, even if it means altering the facts to meet our needs.

Even the slightest movement away from honesty can bring you light years away from the person whom you are, and the attributes you are so desperately trying to connect with. In all the world, there is no battle greater than the one you will wage inside yourself. Nothing is more difficult than brutal honesty—absolutely nothing.

I'm defining "brutal honesty" as *personal truthfulness that is void of defensive thoughts and behaviors, and which tenaciously seeks the facts, regardless of the way they make you feel.* This means that you are willing to face the facts, whatever they may be. The facts are the facts—period. You must never stop looking for the facts—all of them. You don't want to miss any of the information that could be crucial to understanding the truth.

Then, there are those feelings of yours. If you are going to be brutally honest and work with information that is factual, you really need to put those tender little feelings of yours on the back burner. It won't kill you, and it will provide you with the ability to focus your attention on the fact-based information you need. Brutal honesty is an all-or-nothing proposition. There is no such thing as being a little bit dishonest, and there are no little white lies. It is important to understand that to gain control over the way you live your life, you must be honest with yourself without reservation, often to the point of discomfort.

## The Heart of the Matter

Gaining control means to connect with the intelligent, factual version of the person you are. You need to connect with information that is factual, even if you don't particularly like it. The moment you tell yourself something is different from the way it really is, you have lost connection with the pertinent facts you need—facts necessary for you to remain in control of yourself, and the situations you must manage in your life. When you lie, or misrepresent the facts, you relinquish your control over what is happening in your life, because you are relying on inaccurate information. So, how do you know if you're being brutally honest with yourself?

## PEELING THE ONION

Let's illustrate becoming brutally honest with yourself by comparing it to the layers of an onion. The first layer consists of onion paper, and the outside skin. There's not much to it, and little of it is usable. It's often discarded. The same holds true for the first level of honesty. This layer is filled with emotion, defenses, and sometimes agendas. It doesn't always have much that's usable. The second layer of the onion causes you to feel somewhat uncomfortable, as both your sense of smell and your eyes are affected. So too the second level of honesty requires that you go deeper, lose some of the emotion, defenses, and agendas, and work with more of those facts that make you feel uncomfortable. Then there's that third level, where the real tears begin, and your nose begins to burn just a bit. Now you're really uncomfortable. This is where you find brutal honesty. You are uncomfortable, period. There are no defenses, no games, no diversions, and your emotions are not controlling your brain. So, the answer to the question is you are uncomfortable, and you are facing the facts, and only the facts.

### The Cover-up

The most common method of avoiding the brutally honest truth about yourself is to transfer the blame to other people or other situations. The human mind does not like to be attacked, and is well equipped to do what it needs to do to ward off any potential threat. So, you blame external forces for your difficulties. This may work for the moment, but it doesn't do anything to help you improve your ability to address your own concerns. Consequently, you will continue to repeat the same mistakes. If you're going to embrace the task at hand, and rid yourself of negative and toxic energy, then you must be brutally honest with yourself.

You must be willing to admit that you are wrong, that you have some flaws, and that change within you does need to occur. To make intelligent changes, you need to accept the facts that exist in your life with sincere and tenacious brutal honesty. If you can do this, you will set the stage for the positive change, which leads to sustained personal growth. When you do make that connection to the person you are, you want it to be with a person wearing no masks; one who is completely open and honest. The potential for change, and ultimately growth, starts there.

People tend to like quick fixes, don't like to be uncomfortable, and rarely want to be told about the need for personal improvement. Brutal honesty, while it is connecting with those not so attractive parts of us, unsympathetically suggests the necessity for additional work. That, we also don't like. We tend to compare ourselves to other people. The last thing we all want is to come up short and feel as though others are either better than we are, or that they have more going on than we do. We do our best to avoid this.

Brutal honesty, and the results that it may yield, seems to put you at a disadvantage, or at least you may feel that way. It begins to strip away that "I'm in control" mask you have created; the one you like to use so that you, and the rest of the world, can't see the real version of who you are. If you don't become honest, you will remain at a disadvantage, and your chances to be happy and fulfilled as your life unfolds will be significantly reduced. Honesty starts internally and then moves its way outward. You will either accept the truth, or you will live through your lies.

## You Have Options

Honesty is a personal process. You don't have to go out and disclose the horrible truth about yourself to the world. The most important part of being honest is to stop looking outside of yourself for the reasons why you are feeling conflict and discomfort. Misrepresenting the truth starts inside you, not from some other person or situation. You have free will, and you are able to respond to situations in your life using any number of plausible options. Your first rule is to keep it about you. Ask yourself:

➤ *What am I thinking?*

➤ *How am I feeling?*

➤ *Where is this feeling or thought I am having coming from?*

This is where you try to take your emotions out of the picture, lay out the facts as they exist, and begin to come to terms with the real information. Remember, no one else is getting this information, so, there's no reason to feel threatened about admitting it.

If you are willing to take a good hard look at yourself, and accept that not so attractive information, with the understanding that you can change what isn't working, you are poised to grow personally, and to connect with the parts of yourself that need to change. You will be doing this with a vital and dynamic process that will be available to you every day of your life. As long as you live, you can achieve the results you desire if the process you are using is robust, honest, and efficient. You start by being brutally honest with yourself.

Honesty, this brutal honesty I am talking about, is an important step in the Process Way of Life. Honesty requires a little less ego than you may be used to. It also requires that you don't formulate conclusions about how you want something to look before you examine the facts relevant to that situation. So, don't tell yourself that something is true before you've looked at *all* the information. Arrive at an understanding about your situation based on honest factual information. It may be uncomfortable initially, but it sets the stage for the confident, capable person you can be.

1. Let go of the honesty you think you have. Make a commitment to go beyond the way you have approached honesty before. Go deeper, and be honest until you feel some discomfort. That's when you know you're arriving at the truth.

2. Try to keep your emotions and your defenses to a minimum. The facts are so important now. Don't let your emotions misrepresent them. You'll see how to do this in Chapter 4.

3. Make being honest all about you. Ask yourself the relevant questions: *What am I thinking, feeling, and where is all this confusion coming from?* Look inside first.

4. Never blame someone else for something you're feeling. Your feelings are your own. They come from you.

5. Try not to go easy on yourself when it comes to facing the truth. Go straight to the facts. The facts will present you with the best way of becoming the happy person you want to be.

6. There is going to be some discomfort as you come to terms with your honest information. This is temporary and necessary if changes are going to be made. Just be as honest with yourself as you can be. Brutal honesty will connect you with parts of yourself you don't like, but change starts there. You can do this.

7. Understand that brutal honesty is a lifelong process. Don't be afraid of it. If you give it a chance, it will become the best friend you will ever have.

## DRIVING IT HOME

How honest you are willing to be with yourself will correlate directly to the amount of happiness you will create in your life. Make a commitment to move past your old definition of honesty. Be willing to accept a bit of discomfort. That's telling you that you're growing. The facts will always be the facts. Learn to love them.

**YOUR DECLARATION IS:** *I am about the truth, and nothing but the truth.*

## ONWARD

Now that you're doing your best to work with the facts, you want to keep your emotions from distorting them, and creating a picture that doesn't represent the facts. It's time to put your intellect ahead of your emotions.

# CHAPTER 4

# I Over E: Brain Power Over Emotional Madness

*In all you do, let the power of your brain precede the storm of your emotions.*

---

**PROCESSES TO EMPLOY:** Brutal Honesty, I Over E, Present/ Understand/Fix, Slowing Down Life's Pace, Emotional Control, Intelligent Decision-Making, Fact-Finding

---

THE MERRIAM-WEBSTER DICTIONARY DEFINES "INTELLECT" as the faculty of reasoning and understanding objectively. It defines "emotion" as a basic natural instinct: the state of mind deriving from circumstance, mood, or relationships with others. One of the most important themes you will see throughout this book comes down to one simple statement: intellect over emotions (I Over E). Your goal is to increase your emotional intelligence—that is, your capacity to be aware of, control, and express your emotions judiciously and appropriately.

As you proceed through this book and engage in the Process Way of Life, I will consistently reinforce that, in any situation that requires you to think and respond, you must apply the actions of the intellect first. When all facts and relevant information have been acquired and properly defined, emotions can then be applied without destroying the presentation of the facts, and in the end, how you address those facts.

# The Primal Pull

Nothing in our lives is more potent than our intellect. Yet, nothing has the power to interrupt the intellectual processes more than our emotions. Emotions often present themselves as primal and impassioned. They arrive without invitation, and almost always have an agenda. Our brains are unique and magnificent processing machines. They can be likened to a high-powered computer on steroids. They operate in milliseconds, and are capable of multitasking routinely.

Emotions are to your brain like a virus is to your computer, even when they're positive. That's because your energy resources are being diverted to sensations that can significantly reduce your brain's ability to organize information. Emotions introduce conflict and confusion, making what was crystal clear appear disorganized and fragmented. Like your computer, your brain has a specific operational format. When it runs true to form, it accurately perceives information, internalizes that information, codes it, and makes it available when you need it.

It's important that the information your brain is going to store for retrieval be error-free. If there's a breakdown in the process, the information will be inaccurate, and it can affect your ability to arrive at efficient solutions. There can be a profound effect on your relationships, employment, your family, and your health. This is because you may be routinely correcting the mistakes you are making since your process of information-gathering has been corrupted.

Your emotions are charged with the task of expressing the way you feel, but they can also direct the way you feel. Sometimes, they can overpower your intellect, even when you know what you're doing isn't the right decision to make. Your emotions can become so strong that you may be willing to make choices that you know will negatively impact your life, but you choose to make them regardless of the consequences. Here's an illustration:

## ROLLING IN THE POISON PATCH

Twenty-two-year-old Jenny is a senior at a small private college. She is a biology major and plans to become a marine biologist when she graduates. Though she is a dean's list student, she is known for making "on the spot" decisions. Her fall semester is nearing its end, and her final exam in Molecular Biology is on Monday. This is one of the more difficult subjects in her major, and requires a significant amount of preparation.

It's Saturday afternoon, and Jenny has planned an evening of study with friends at the library. That afternoon, a student she likes has asked her to accompany him to a party. The party starts at 8 o'clock, and will probably run into the early hours on Sunday morning. Jenny knows that if she doesn't spend the night studying at the library, her chances of passing the exam decrease, but she really likes this student.

A review of the facts tells her that the correct decision is to disregard the invitation, and go to the library. Jenny understands what she is supposed to do, and then finds herself experiencing the conflict we all have when we want to do something, but sound information tells us to move in a different direction.

Jenny decides on a compromise. She'll study all afternoon, blow off the study session, and go to the party. Then, she'll spend all of Sunday studying with friends for the exam. She attends the party, but when Sunday comes, she has a horrible post-party headache, and can't concentrate on her notes. Expect the fallout from Jenny's decision to be a lower grade on her exam. She must now suffer the consequences.

So, when your emotions override your intellect, you can create serious problems for yourself. What should have been a higher grade on Jenny's exam was willfully sacrificed in favor of a fun-filled evening of party fun. She paid a steep price for her decision. If you roll in the poison patch, expect the rash.

## The Internal Battleground

We often find ourselves having a difficult time separating the intellect's version of the facts from those that are being redesigned by the emotions. As you proceed in life, you will make your best decisions by using accurate information that is factually based. If that information is being tainted by your emotions, you put yourself at a disadvantage regarding your ability to problem-solve, and reach efficient solutions.

There is the factual version, and there is the version which your emotions help you create. Rarely are they complementary. This occurs because, as you are attempting to understand the information that is being presented to your brain, your emotions may be operating at a level of strength that supersedes that of your intellect. This makes the information look different, usually in tune with the way you want it to look, and as a result, your decision-making capabilities can be compromised. Call it putting your emotional cart before your intellectual horse.

Before you allow your emotions to impact the information being presented, you need to learn how to hold on to those emotions, at least until you can gain an accurate understanding of the facts. If you attempt to alter the facts based on emotional needs or are overreacting to what is happening, you can lose sight of the information you need to efficiently address the situation. This isn't to say that you cannot be emotional or that you cannot express your emotions. It simply says that you want to give your brain enough time to present and interpret the facts before your emotions take over. You just want to have the correct information before you make important decisions that may significantly alter the course of your life.

## Powering Down—
## 7 Practical Steps to Reduce Your Emotions

In many of the chapters throughout the book, including this one, I will be telling you that you need to get your emotions out of things, to try to calm down, or put your intellect before your emotions.

What follows are some practical steps you can take to help you start the process. You'll be directed back to Chapter 4, and these steps, many times throughout the book when I'm queuing you to put your emotions aside. This will help remind you of the steps you can use to make that happen. Here are those steps:

1. Hit your pause button: if you can, stop for a moment. This will give you some time to decide what you want to do next.

2. Try to remove yourself from the situation. This also gives you time to think about what's going on, and make a decision about what to do.

3. Emotions can have you going too fast. Take slow, deliberate, deep breaths. This allows your body to readjust, and gives you enough mental focus to make your decision. I'll be discussing some breathing techniques in the next chapter.

4. Identify your emotions. Ask yourself *What am I feeling, and where is this feeling coming from?* This will make what feels unknown a bit more identifiable. It's easier to deal with something that you can identify than something which is vague and undefined.

5. Try to visualize yourself being a bit calmer. This can help you remove your attention from the emotions you are feeling.

6. Talk to someone. It's much easier to define what's going on by talking it over with someone you trust.

7. This may be the most important step. Make a conscious decision to stop, think, and respond. Say the words: I stop; I think; I respond. Breathe; then, make your decision.

Reducing emotions, and learning how to express your intellect first, is one of those difficult behaviors to change. However, if you keep working on it, using the 7 Practical Steps, and applying them in your life as often as you can, you will begin to see changes; albeit small changes. That, however, is where big change begins.

## ⏱ TIME TO TAKE ACTION

1. Go slow. Few facts are accurately registered in the brain while it is under pressure. Slow down and allow yourself enough time to gather the facts, exactly as they exist. Start with your breathing. I'm going to look at reducing the pace of your life in Chapter 5.

2. Acquire accurate facts for each and every situation in your life. Do your best to focus on getting the facts, and address your emotions later. Writing them down can help.

3. Emotions are agenda experts. Ask yourself if you have some type of an agenda, or if you want the facts to lead to some desired conclusion.

4. At times, you will continue to become emotional before you give yourself enough time to think. When this happens, slow down a bit, and remove yourself from the situation. Take a walk, or anything that can distract you from your emotions. Return to the facts after you have had some time to clear your head.

5. Your emotions are going to enter any situation you are involved in. Try to make that occur after you organize the facts. There is nothing wrong with the way you feel about a situation, but try to make it how you feel about the facts first.

6. If you are going to make a decision that is not in your best interest, and if you know that this decision is wrong, understand the consequences, and be willing to accept them. Don't blame others or some unrelated set of circumstances. You did it. You own it. You fix it.

7. If you are having a problem slowing down, and removing your emotions from the situation, ask someone for help.

 **DRIVING IT HOME**

It will take time to reverse the process from emotion over intellect to intellect over emotion. For now, understand that your intellect needs to be expressed first, and work with the 7 Practical Steps. This will help set the stage for all those great things we're going to be doing as the Process Way of Life unfolds.

**YOUR DECLARATION IS**: *My intellect comes first; my emotions follow.*

 **ONWARD**

I've mentioned slowing down several times, but how do you go about doing that? It's time to take your life off speed dial, and give yourself enough time to process the information you need to be healthy and happy.

◇◇◇◇◇◇◇◇◇◇◇◇

# CHAPTER 5

# Slowing Down Life's Pace to Be Happy

*Slow life's pace. Take time to get back to yourself, and understand what's happening in your life.*

---

**PROCESSES TO EMPLOY:** Brutal Honesty, I Over E, Present/ Understand/Fix, Slowing Down Life's Pace, Incremental Forward Movement, Patience

---

SPEED AND MULTITASKING HAVE BECOME A CONDITION of living that defines almost everything we do. With an unbridled passion, so many of us actively pursue this chaotic, revved-up style of life. Many of us live at a pace that can compromise the quality of our lives, and destroy our health.

It's easy to normalize, and even embrace this accelerated pace, adding even more stimulation and intensity to our lives. Many of us use artificial stimulants in the belief that they will somehow allow us to do more, to feel more, and to feel better about ourselves. We often demand this accelerated pace in our own lives, and from everyone else.

We live in a world where an increasingly large number of people are being prescribed medications for depression and anxiety, and street drug use is at epidemic proportions. The divorce rate is higher now than it's ever been, and for many, suicide has now become a "logical" way out a life that is anxiety-ridden, and often out of control. We continue to push ourselves to go from point A to point B as fast as we can, seemingly unable to decelerate long enough to catch our breath. We seem to be going nowhere, fast.

## Speed Kills

Circadian rhythms—forces inside us that keep our bodies regulated and in balance—no longer operate efficiently, and we continue to use artificial means to regulate us physically, emotionally, and psychologically. Our daily biorhythms, smaller rhythms in our bodies that keep us regulated during the day, are routinely compromised. For many of us, artificial means are the only way to keep our bodies functioning as we dash through our frenzied, open-throttle lives.

The human body wasn't designed to operate at such an accelerated pace. We humans are a species designed for periods of action, followed by periods of rest. We are at our best when we have the proper amount of sleep, followed by a day that is lived at a moderate pace, and is not so physically and/or emotionally challenging that we become empty and exhausted by sundown.

This is another area where we need to apply conscious thought to direct our lives. The rule of thumb is: the faster we live life, the less thought we will apply to doing so. When life's pace becomes so accelerated that we don't have time to think about what we're doing and how we're doing it, we are putting ourselves at the mercy of a style of living that can only hurt us.

Living this way can actually bring us to the point that we don't understand what a healthy life pace is, let alone how to live that way. Below, I've included a table that compares a healthy life pace with one that is unhealthy. This will help you examine the pace of your own life.

| Healthy Pace | Unhealthy Pace |
|---|---|
| Monitors life pace | Life lived on autopilot |
| Takes time for self | Constantly on the go |
| Adopts a healthy personal life pace | Runs at others' pace |
| Prioritizes time | Little established order to life |
| Lives by natural flow | Relies on artificial stimulants |
| Conscious focus is on keeping pace slow | Harried pace seems normal |
| Schedules personal time | No or little personal time scheduled |
| Evaluates and makes changes in life schedule | Does not evaluate and make changes in life schedule |

## Easy Does It

Nothing good happens fast. It is imperative that you slow down the pace of your day by simplifying your daily routine. This will allow you to apply some rational thought to your life. Here are some practical suggestions:

➤ Make a list of what you need to do today; one that you can accomplish without undue stress. Don't over-schedule yourself.

➤ Schedule some downtime into your day. For example, try to schedule a 15-minute break into your daily routine.

➤ Stop being everyone's "go to" person. Let them handle their own responsibilities.

➤ Wake up 10 minutes earlier than usual to practice a soothing self-care ritual.

➤ Prioritize your day. Ask yourself what "absolutely has to be done." Do just that.

➤ Get off autopilot. Ask yourself how fast you need to go. Going fast and autopilot living go hand-in-hand.

- Practice deep breathing, meditation, or yoga; exercise, pray, or read a book.

- Avoid artificial forms of physical accelerants like energy drinks, sugar, caffeine, and other amphetamines.

If you don't learn to slow the pace of your life, there is no way you are going to embrace the changes I'm talking about in this book. Here's a very simple example to illustrate this:

If you run around the room while someone is talking to you, you won't be able to hear much of what they say. On the other hand, if you slow your pace to a walk, the chances of hearing everything they say dramatically increases. So it is with the pace of your life. If you want to feel good and make changes that improve the quality of your life, you're going to have to slow down enough to understand what's going on around you. The Process Way of Life, and in the end, your happiness, depends on your willingness to decelerate the pace of your life.

Any goal worth achieving is worth enjoying. This self-defeating, over-accelerated way of living is an abomination that can lead to no other end but self-destruction. If you want peace of mind, slow down long enough to understand what that is, how you can acquire it, and incorporate it into your life. Take the time to understand who you are, and how to enjoy your life.

## TIME TO TAKE ACTION

1. Slow down, slow down, and slow down. You don't need to crawl, but you really do need to stop running. Follow the suggested activities on page 37 to get started. Do whatever it takes to infuse your life with some slow-paced quality time.

2. Regulate your body. Your body has everything you need for you to be healthy. Stop filling it with artificial stimulants and other drugs to accelerate the pace of your life. Return to the natural pace that was meant for your body.

3. When possible, remove yourself from people, places, and circumstances that demand a pace of life you simply don't need to maintain. No happy ending has ever been achieved by trying to keep up with the Joneses. I'll be discussing removing toxic people in Chapter 19.

4. Evaluate the pace of your life daily. Several times each day, monitor the way you feel physically and emotionally, and what you are thinking about. Then, make adjustments to more efficiently address your life pace for that day, if necessary.

 ## DRIVING IT HOME

Little in life is appreciated on the run. Do take care of business, but slow down enough to appreciate the gifts that life is offering you. Take your life off speed dial. Reduce the pace at which you've been living, and come back to yourself.

**YOUR DECLARATION IS**: *I will slow down, I will catch my breath, I will enjoy my life.*

 ## ONWARD

To live a full life, having trust in yourself is essential. Your trust in yourself will increase as you begin to live according to the Process Way of Life. You will identify your own capabilities, and learn to trust the processes that are already inside you. I'll explain how to learn to trust yourself by trusting the processes in the next chapter.

◇◇◇◇◇◇◇◇◇◇◇◇

# CHAPTER 6

# Trust the Process and Learn to Trust Yourself

*Connect to the processes that are already inside you. To learn to trust the Process Way of Life is to learn to trust yourself.*

---

**PROCESSES TO EMPLOY:** Brutal Honesty, I Over E, Present/ Understand/Fix, Slowing Down Life's Pace, Incremental Forward Movement, Life on Life's Terms, Life's Natural Flow, Keeping Life Simple, Trust

---

EVERYTHING IN LIFE IS A PROCESS. In fact, all of life can be broken down into smaller processes, each charged with a specific task that maintains life, and helps to enhance the quality of life. Human beings, being natural, organic life forms, are governed by biological processes that maintain our bodies, such as: digestion, growth, excretion, respiration, and reproduction. These processes must be carried out according to a specific protocol so that our bodies can survive and run efficiently.

Processes are not limited to the way our bodies work. They are also involved in our everyday lives. If you look at any part of your life, you will find that there is some type of process governing it, regardless of how insignificant it may seem to be. The simpler activities like making something to eat to the more complex life-changing enterprises are all governed by their own specific set of processes. Defining and understanding these processes and their natural flow, and learning to bring that natural flow into your daily endeavors, can help you more efficiently attain the results you desire.

Let's look at a simple example. A man has owned his business for twenty years, and now, as he approaches age fifty, he wants to begin the process of bringing his son into his business. He has two options to accomplish this:

1. He can bring his son directly into the administrative level, and eventually turn the business over to him.

2. He can bring his son into the business on the ground level. There, he will learn what the hourly workers do, and to troubleshoot at the factory level. He will also encounter the workday with his employees on a more personal level, and he will learn the administrative part of the business.

In the second example, the young man learned all the processes that would be relevant to running his father's business efficiently when his time comes. He will be more experienced at the factory level, more understanding of his employees' needs, and understand what to do when things go wrong. He will also be more efficient when it comes to administrative duties, and forecasting the company's future needs.

So, the process was first identified (the father realized that his son needed to learn everything about the business). Next, the father designed a plan that would teach his son to successfully run, and eventually lead the company. Then, when his son is ready he could assume control of the business. By doing this, the father was able to trust his son with the business, and the young man was able to trust his abilities as he moved forward. Trusting the process made all this happen.

## Mother Nature Says

So, there are natural processes that need to occur to increase the probability of success. We humans, in general, like to obtain what we want, the way we want it, and when we want it. Unfortunately, this has little to do with the way life naturally works, as you will see as I discuss life's natural flow in Chapter 9. When you attempt to acquire something without paying attention to the processes that govern it, you lose valuable information to efficiently bring your endeavor to fruition. These processes will be essential as you move into the more sophisticated and complex levels of your endeavors.

Every aspect of your life depends on the understanding and definition of the processes associated with it. There is nothing you will do that doesn't find itself associated with some process. As you become adept at understanding, defining, and incorporating the processes I am discussing into the way you live life, these processes will strengthen your movement toward your own internal balance.

## The 7 Steps to Process Implementation

1. Present your goal or objective.

2. Slow down enough to gather the facts you need.

3. Break your facts down into the smaller processes that can make your plan work.

4. Prioritize your process-based factual information.

5. Organize the information into a step-by-step plan.

6. Go slow, and build in some time to reassess and adjust the plan when necessary.

7. Execute your step-by-step plan.

As I mentioned in the introduction to this book, to become balanced physically, intellectually, emotionally, and spiritually is your most important goal. It is the holy grail; the central force of everything I am teaching. When you understand the concept of internal balance and how to define, interpret, and organize the processes that are necessary to live a balanced life, you will set the stage for a style of life that can prepare you for everything you will experience as your new world unfolds.

The processes I am presenting you with are the key components that will help you arrive at this balanced state of living. You can flip back to page 7 to remind yourself of what they are, and how I'm using them. Remember, they are already in you, and you possess the ability to understand them, and incorporate them into your life. When you do, you will redefine who you are, and you will learn to trust both the processes, and yourself. For now, simply focus on trusting the notion that there is a process-guided program that can help you make the changes in your life that are so important to you. You're going to learn to live your life by the processes that naturally define it. You will grow through them, and you will be happy.

 **TIME TO TAKE ACTION**

1. Take some time to look at everything you do during a typical day. Identify the little processes—that is, those little actions it took to achieve them. Don't be concerned about how trivial or insignificant they may seem. Break that activity down to the simplest steps that are involved in the process. There will be many. For example, Take brushing your teeth. You will grab your toothbrush. Then you take the toothpaste, remove the cap, apply the toothpaste to the toothbrush, turn on the water, dip the toothbrush, bring it to your mouth, and brush your teeth. There will be more. Try to identify them.

2. At the end of the day, make a list of all the important tasks you completed. Now, identify the smaller processes that made them happen, just as I did in step one. This will give you an idea of how many smaller processes are involved throughout your day. It will also show you how well you mastered all of them. Being able to identify and define your capabilities is a huge asset in life, and identifying smaller steps creates the pathway to making this happen. Remember, you're going to be working with far greater processes as we proceed. The simple exercises will prepare your mind for what's to come in the program.

3. Referring back to our example of the businessman and his son, the father identified his processes, defined them, and then implemented a program that could efficiently teach his son about the business. By doing this, he trusted his plan, himself, and eventually his son. Make a working plan for tomorrow. Write your plan down. Include everything you are doing from the time you awake until bedtime. Then, identify the processes you will need to make all of this happen. By doing so, you are beginning to define and trust your processes, and how you use them. You don't need to do this every day; just long enough to understand how your daily processes work.

 ## DRIVING IT HOME

It's important to learn to understand and become trusting of all the smaller processes associated with everything you do each day. By doing so, you will begin to connect with and trust the processes inside you, and yourself. This sets the stage for the more sophisticated process-oriented growth you will be undertaking very soon. You are starting small, but the bigger process growth is about to begin. To trust the Process Way of Life *is* to learn to trust yourself.

**YOUR DECLARATION IS**: *I will trust the process; I will trust myself.*

 ## ONWARD

Life is a journey, and you are applying everything you are learning to help create that marvelous trip through life moment by moment. The next chapter will explain how to enjoy the wonderful journey that is your life.

# CHAPTER 7

# Life Is a Journey: Love Yours

*Every moment of your life is precious. Learn to be happy day-by-day, moment-by-moment, as your life journey unfolds.*

---

**PROCESSES TO EMPLOY**: Brutal Honesty, I Over E, Present/ Understand/Fix, Slowing Down Life's Pace, Incremental Forward Movement, Journey Living, Living in the Moment, One-Day-at-a-Time Living, Reduction of Destination Living

---

**WHEN WE CONSIDER THE SUM TOTAL OF** our entire human experience, we spend a few short moments coming into the world, and a few short moments leaving it. Almost our entire human experience is spent on the journey that starts immediately after birth and ends immediately before death. So, between these two existential life bookends, we will experience one precious moment after another, each holding its own unique purpose, and together, these moments will create the story of our lives.

As we travel, moment to moment, and experience to experience, our life journey can be hard to appreciate. It's often difficult to get excited about what happens in our routine daily lives. So, we introduce destinations: exciting events that help provide more definition to our lives, making us feel better about our existence. Inherent in the design for a destination is the assumption that we will be happier when we arrive there. If that were not the case, and there were no payoff, we might choose not to make the trip.

Having destinations in our lives can be positive for us. The concern is that we might define these destinations as more important than the rest of our lives. If we are overemphasizing small segments of our life journey, what does that say about the rest of our life's timeline? Life is really about our entire journey. It's about what we are experiencing every moment of our lives.

## They're Not All Bad

The concern about destinations is really in the way you approach them. You should be happy in all the routine moments of your life—even the ones that also include work, mundane chores, responsibilities, and general family life. This is where almost all of life is lived, so it's important that these moments, which define the bulk of your life journey, also bring you happiness. When you can say that you can be content without exciting destinations, and that your life, that is your day-by-day journey is a wonderful place to be, you are truly happy.

It's important to understand that people who invest their time being happy along the way usually discover that life's simple moments are the best. They consistently do their best to be happy in all the moments of their lives. It's a wonderful way to live.

Destination-oriented people often have difficulty with the in-between periods. Without destinations, life is often perceived as uneventful and monotonous. For destination thinkers, having exciting landing spots all too often becomes their way of defining life. There's nothing wrong with planning for exciting times. You just want to be sure that all the in-between times have the potential to make you feel good about yourself, your life, and the people in it.

Journey-oriented people enjoy the entire process. These are moments passing on their life's timeline, and they don't want to miss any of them. It's loving your life—all of it, not just the "fun parts."

I'm not saying that having destinations is a problem. It's only problematic when the in-between times seem to be missing something for you. The following table presents the difference between journey living and destination living.

# JOURNEY VERSUS DESTINATION LIVING

| Journey Living | Destination Living |
|---|---|
| Love all the moments of their lives | Life is lived around exciting times |
| Can have fun during the mundane times | Mundane times seem challenging |
| Enjoy making routine times more fun | Have difficulty making in-between times fun |
| Consciously appreciate every second of life | Become impatient waiting for excitement |
| Much easier to please | Tend to be more demanding |
| Can enjoy life on life's terms | Like to be more in control of life's terms |
| Love the simple life | Love to add complexity to life |
| Enjoy destinations, but don't need them | Need destinations to define life as happy |
| May or may not have a bucket list | Bucket list is essential |
| Can go slow in life | "Slow" can get old |

## Who's Who, Here?

So, how do you know if you are a destination or journey person? Here are the important questions:

1. Could you be happy with your life if it did not include exciting destination spots?

2. Do you have as much fun during the more routine times in your life as you do at exciting destinations?

3. Do you enjoy making mundane times more fun?

4. Do you consciously appreciate every second of your life?

5. Are you easy to please, even when there's nothing exciting happening in your life?

6. Do you enjoy life on life's terms, that is, without trying to alter them to meet unnecessary desires?

7. Do you love the simple life?

8. Can you say that you enjoy destinations, but don't need them to be happy?

9. Can you do without a bucket list to have something to look forward to?

10. Can you go slow in life, and be happy at that pace?

If you can answer yes to most of these questions, you are more inclined to be a journey person. If you answered no to most of them, you are probably a destination person.

Journey-oriented people will say that they would like to see that future event come to fruition, but they would still be happy if it doesn't happen. Journey-oriented people will also set goals; however, what they are experiencing in the moment they are living in is equally as important as the destination. In fact, it adds to the exhilaration of the destination.

Journey-oriented people know that achieving the goal may, in some fashion, improve the quality of their lives, but they do not define it as an absolute need. They trust that about themselves. They are happy in the moment they're living in, and love to share those moments with those close to them. For journey-oriented people, every moment of their lives is a destination, in and of itself; a pure and uncomplicated fraction of time to be fully appreciated.

If you refer back to the journey versus destination table, those who love the journey would seem to be more at ease with themselves. They work from within and bring a more peaceful approach to life, to others, and to their external surroundings. They require much less from those external surroundings, which allows them to be happier with whatever is happening in their lives in each moment, and consequently with themselves.

Destination people have a different approach to life. Much of their happiness has its roots in the external environment. They routinely seek out information and experiences that are external to them, so they may feel better about their lives. Those who live their lives gravitating from one destination to another, by definition, are relying on external sources to be happy. They often find it difficult to connect with their own internal resources, so they routinely seek external energy to make them happy.

People who are focusing on being happy moment by moment in their journey through life are typically more emotionally self-sufficient, and usually need less than their destination counterparts. Those who love their life journey moment to moment don't spend so much time focused on something outside of themselves, so they are typically more in control internally, and are less dependent people than their destination friends.

There is nothing wrong with setting goals in life. They can make life more interesting and more fulfilling. Understanding life's simple pleasures, living moment to moment, and being confident internally, however, is an empowering way to live life. It helps you require less from unpredictable future destinations.

The important takeaway here is that most of us do look forward to exciting destinations, and even to parts of our day or week when something special is going to happen. You, however, will enhance your own process journey when you understand how to make all the moments of your life special. When you think about it, would you rather spend your time looking forward to something you hope is going to happen, or would you like to be someone who is perfectly content in the moment you are living in?

In the end, when your time on this earth has come full circle, you can look back and know that you enjoyed the vast majority of the beautiful gift that was your life. Do set goals, and enjoy your time at the destinations, but never make them more important than your day-to-day life. Your life's clock is ticking. Enjoy it one tick at a time.

 **TIME TO TAKE ACTION**

1. Ask yourself this simple question: *Am I happy enough in my life that I can do without exciting destinations?* This question allows you to appraise how you would feel about your life if there were no exciting destinations to look forward to.

2. Destinations can be an important part of your life, but interpret them as goals, that is, something you can systematically accomplish, not just something to look forward to. Define what you have to do each day to realize your goal. Include it in your "things to do today" list, and enjoy the process of working to achieve it, along with everything else you are doing that day. I'll be discussing turning destinations into goals in Chapter 25.

3. Make a conscious decision to enjoy as many moments of your day as you can. Regardless of the task, the people you are with, or any other variables, keep your mind focused on the moment you are living in, and make that one count.

4. Refer back to the questions which help you to define yourself as either a journey or destination person. Make some changes in your life so that it may more closely coincide with the journey way of living.

 **DRIVING IT HOME**

Destinations can be good, but treat them as goals; something that you are going to define, plan for, and work toward each day, along with everything else going on in your life that day. Make all the moments of your life precious to you. Love them, and live them that way. Stay in the present, and live life one precious second at a time. Love and live today with all your heart.

**YOUR DECLARATION IS**: *I will love my life journey, every moment, every breath.*

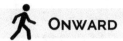 ## ONWARD

There are 86,400 seconds in each day. That's a lot of opportunities to live in the moment. Next, I'm going to show you how to apply your journey-oriented approach to living in the moment.

◇◇◇◇◇◇◇◇◇◇◇◇◇

# CHAPTER 8

# Living in the Moment: The Practical Application

*Say goodbye to your past and plan for your future, but understand that you only have control of the present moment. Focus your energies there.*

**PROCESSES TO EMPLOY:** Brutal Honesty, I Over E, Present/ Understand/Fix, Slowing Down Life's Pace, Keeping Life Simple, Living in the Moment, Journey Living, One-Day-at-a-Time Living, Reduction of Destination Living, Settling Past Issues

BEFORE OUR MINDS BECOME DISCIPLINED ENOUGH TO remain focused in the moment, we find ourselves moving back and forth between what has happened, and what we are anticipating will happen. This energy could be more efficiently used if we spend it focusing on what is happening *now*.

We all have past experiences. Some of those experiences are good, and some are not so good. Focusing on them uses resources we need to efficiently function in today. People and events from our past, and those which have yet to happen, need to be placed into a perspective that does not hinder us from moving forward. If this doesn't happen, we will continue to redirect the energy we need to function today to times and places that have no life in the present.

To help you stay in the moment, you need to understand the concept of internal balance. As I mentioned earlier, living life in balance means giving equal attention to our *physical, intellectual, emotional, and spiritual* attributes. Balancing these four attributes creates a power source that will assist us in all aspects of our lives. Here's how:

## Balance for Beginners

Let's start with the *physical*. Think about a time when you were stressed over some past experiences, or when you were worrying about some potential future event. As the level of stress becomes more potent, you can feel your body tightening, and things begin to move a bit faster. Stress causes physical changes, so it would make sense to do something to minimize the physical acceleration that coincides with stressful events. When you decelerate your physical response to something that causes you to feel anxious, you can provide yourself with an opportunity to think more clearly and with less emotion.

The first step to slow your body down is to focus on your breathing. When you become stressed, your breathing patterns change, becoming faster and shallower. Altering how you breathe in anxious or stressful situations helps you stay focused on what is currently happening. Slowing your breathing and taking deeper, more deliberate breaths will help you in two ways:

1. It causes your body to decelerate so you can gain more control of how you are feeling physically.

2. It automatically causes your mind to refocus on something you are doing in the very moment: your breathing. This then helps you to increase your control over the moment you are living in.

By starting with a physical approach, you are attacking the problem at its most rudimentary point. Adjusting your breathing is not a complex, sophisticated exercise. You simply redirect your attention to breathing slowly and more deliberately. Make yourself comfortable. You can sit down and relax, slowly walk around your home, or even lie down. Your only concern should be to focus your attention on your breathing in the very moment you are doing it. Try to breathe slowly, and you will notice your body starting to relax.

## Get Your Brain Involved

Now that your slower breaths have given you an opportunity to refocus your conscious attention, redirect your *intellectual* energy toward what is occurring right now, and tell yourself, consciously, to refocus on the present. You may say things like *That hasn't come yet, so I'm not going to think about that now.* You might look at past events and say *That's over, I can't change what occurred, and I need to move on.*

This step allows you to gain a bit more control over how you are thinking and feeling, because it helps you make a conscious choice. *I will not think about that.* Not only does making statements like these redirect your energies, it's the first step in helping you to empower yourself, and not feel victimized by what has occurred or may occur.

Every life change starts with small steps. Saying *I will not think about that* is a small step, but it's such an important one to take. You have been living your life by using phrases that reinforce anxiety for a long time, like *I can't do this*, and *I'm not good enough.* Those phrases redirect your attention back to the pain from the past, and forward to apprehensive future situations. Your mind has been trained to do this. It happens to all of us, and as you continue to talk yourself into the moment you are living in, the power the past and the future have over you will begin to diminish. It just takes some time. Keep repeating the process. Little by little, it starts to work. I'll discuss how to use your personal language in greater detail in Chapter 23.

## Marking Your Territory, and Talking It Up

With your breathing slower, and your attention consciously focused on the present moment, we turn our attention to the *emotional* part of our plan. I call this step "marking the moment." By marking the moment, I am talking about a two-step process that begins by identifying (marking) and focusing on something you see in the present moment. It could be a person, an object, or anything you can focus on in the moment. By doing this, you are directing your attention to something right in front of you, something that is occurring in the moment. You want to make the living-in-the-moment experience a positive one, so identify something you like, and focus your attention there.

Once you have identified the mark, you want to *enhance your mark*. This simply means to take what you have focused your attention on, something that may make you feel good, and assign positive value to it. You can do this by telling yourself how much you like it, or some positive way it makes you feel. For example, you might say *I really like the way that makes me feel,* or *I love when I do that.* "Talking it up" makes the moment you are living in a more attractive place to be.

This is contrary to what you usually do. You usually reinforce the negative moments. You tell yourself how much you don't like something, or how bad it makes you feel. So, you've already been marking and enhancing. All you are going to do now is switch your energy and attention to doing this in a positive way, that is, to something you like in the moment you are living in. You will find that this positive linguistic reversal can have a positive influence, just as it's negative counterpart caused negative thoughts and feelings for you.

## The Higher Power

The next step focuses attention on the *spiritual* part of our being. This is a part of life that some people will champion rigorously, while others feel more comfortable with an "in moderation" approach. Others deny it altogether. If you embrace the spiritual part of yourself, or are, at least, willing to look at it, there can be appreciable benefits. You can use this step by saying prayers to God, or you may choose to embrace meditation or mindfulness. I am talking about being connected to the spirit within you to keep you grounded in the present moment. There is a spirit that resides within you, and exerts its influence in the here and now. It moves through you, and everything you do, and in every moment you are living. Your spirituality is where you will find your inner peace

One of the most simple and straightforward ways to connect with your spirituality is to learn simple meditation. Meditation helps you move to a relaxed level of consciousness where you can experience life in a more balanced state. While you may have heard that even a few minutes of meditation helps, I advise you to meditate for about twenty minutes a day. Twenty minutes of meditation is how long it takes for your body to efficiently reduce your heart rate and begin to feel more tranquil. Some of the practical gains from meditation are:

1. Increased immune function
2. Decreased pain
3. Spiritual connectivity
4. Increased positive emotion
5. Decreased depression
6. Decreased anxiety
7. Increased mental clarity

The easiest way to incorporate meditation into your life is to combine it with your breathing exercises. Practice by sitting quietly and breathe slowly. Then, try to clear your mind—that is, focus on absolutely nothing. As thoughts come into your mind, redirect your mind back to your breathing. This will help you "exist" in the moment, since you are not focusing on anything but your breathing.

Some people find using a mantra beneficial to help them keep their mind clear. A mantra is simply a sound that has no linguistic connection; no attachment to anything of meaning in your life. You don't have to use a mantra, but if you are having trouble clearing your mind and keeping it clear, a mantra can help. The traditional example of a mantra is *om*, repeated as you exhale. You can also create your own unconnected sound. While you meditate, say the mantra out loud or silently. When you become proficient at meditation, you will also begin to connect to the spiritual part of your life. You will feel more refreshed, have more energy, and your mind will find it easier to stay in the moment.

Our lives are comprised of energy that is expressed physically, intellectually, emotionally, and spiritually. So, it's important to learn to direct your energy to all of them in the moment you are living in.

➤ Do the breathing exercises.

➤ Use positive language.

➤ Mark and enhance your life moments.

➤ Try prayer or meditation.

You will know you are making progress because you will feel less rushed, less stressed, and less conflicted; you'll start to feel more inner peace. You will also realize that you are more productive in the present.

 **TIME TO TAKE ACTION**

1. Physically, learn to adjust your breathing. Try to breathe slower and more deliberately. Here's a simple breathing exercise:

   ➤ Exhale completely through your mouth.

   ➤ Close your mouth and inhale quietly through your nose to a count of five.

   ➤ Hold your breath for a count of five.

   ➤ Exhale completely through your mouth to a count of five.

   ➤ Now, repeat the cycle until you feel yourself becoming more relaxed.

2. Intellectually, use self-coaching to verbally train your mind to stay in the moment. Do so by saying, "I'm not going to think about that now," or "That's over, I can't change what's occurred, and I need to move on."

3. Emotionally, identify and mark your present experience. Make it more attractive to live in by "talking up" what you are experiencing there.

4. Spiritually, use meditation or prayer to connect with your spiritual side. Incorporating either of them while you are controlling your breathing allows you to go deeper inside yourself, and that's where you will find your spirituality.

The Process Way of Life is going to take time to fully develop in your daily life. To maximize the benefits of the foregoing exercises, it's important to stick with them and perform them regularly, on a daily basis. You will feel the benefits if you stay consistent for a month. Make a commitment to be consistent, and be willing to do the work that it takes to make the changes that are important to you.

 ## DRIVING IT HOME

This in-the-moment approach helps you to naturally flow into and be comfortable in your present life—the moment you are living in. There, you can learn to live and be happy without being invaded by thoughts and feelings from places and times that have no life and no purpose in the present.

**YOUR DECLARATION IS:** *I live where my life is happening.*

 ## ONWARD

*Living life* in the moment is a very self-empowering way to live. It keeps you focusing on what is happening where and when it is happening; when you have the most control over it. Another natural flow is staying in the day we are living in. That's where your energy is best spent. I'm going to explore the importance of staying in today next.

◇◇◇◇◇◇◇◇◇◇◇◇◇

# CHAPTER 9

# The Backward/ Forward Principle

## The Importance of Staying in Today

*The past is dead, and the future does not yet exist. Stop breathing life into frames of time you cannot control.*

---

**PROCESSES TO EMPLOY:** Brutal Honesty, I Over E, Present/ Understand/Fix, Slowing Down Life's Pace, Journey Living, Keeping Life Simple, Living in the Moment, One-Day-at-a-Time Living, Reduction of Destination Living, Settling Past Issues

---

I DISCUSSED HOW STAYING IN THE MOMENT is so important. Staying in today, and keeping your mind focused on what you can do today, is equally as important. It requires concentration that cannot become disrupted by events that have occurred or may occur. You cannot change the past, and you cannot live in a time that has not yet arrived.

As I presented in Chapter 4, emotions can have a significant effect on how healthy you are, and how efficiently you can address what is occurring in your life. One-day-at-a-time living keeps you grounded in the day in which you are living, so that your emotions don't move back and forth robbing you of the energy you need to address what is happening today. Let's look at what might happen if we have something important to address today, but we are distracted by experiences from people and events which cannot be addressed today.

## THE HUMAN PING PONG BALL

Sophia is forty-three years old, and has been married for twenty-one years. She has been working as a marketing associate in an advertising firm for ten years. Sophia's parents divorced when she was thirteen, and she has a tenuous relationship with her mother.

Sophia has an important presentation to make at a partners' meeting tomorrow. That afternoon, Sophia's mother, someone who wants things her way, calls her. She needs help with something that is not an emergency and, as usual, makes Sophia feel guilty for past events to get her to do what she wants her to do, *now*. The whole situation makes Sophia anxious and angry. Later that evening, as Sophia is trying to review her presentation, her husband comes home and reports that they are laying off people where he works. Though he thinks he's safe, he could spend some time out of work. This could create some financial concerns.

Sophia needs all her energy to focus on the presentation, but now she is doing a time-oriented balancing act. Although the presentation is receiving some attention, so are the other situations: neither having anything to do with today.

If Sophia continues to give these situations attention, her presentation will undoubtedly suffer. This is an example of the *backward/forward principle*. Sophia, needing to focus on today, is now pulled by her past (backward) and a potential future event (forward). Her mind will continue to go backward and forward while she focuses on the present, that is, the report.

To resolve the situation, Sophia needs to tell her mother that she is involved in something that requires her attention, and she will call her tomorrow, after the presentation is done. Her mother may continue in her attempts to push her, but she can only be effective if Sophia allows this to happen. This is a boundary issue, one that Sophia must defend. I'll be discussing boundaries in Chapter 21.

As far as her husband's situation is concerned, she has no control over it, and worrying will not change it. She can be supportive with her husband, and then they need to agree that they will wait and see what happens. By taking care of these two situations, Sophia has the time to focus on what needs to be done today, *in her present life.*

Focusing on today allows you to live life to the fullest, be more efficient in your daily life, and it keeps your emotions in check. This is so important to your happiness, and your general health, and introduces another important theme of this chapter: energy distribution.

## Put It Where It Belongs

For every action produced in the human body, there is a corresponding amount of energy that must be distributed to fuel that action. This energy powers the body and the mind, and moves them toward the desired outcome. Everything you think and do uses energy.

➤ First, there is physical energy. Everything you do physically, whether it is something as simple as turning the pages while reading a book to the rigors associated with physical labor, requires energy.

➤ Then, there is intellectual energy. Here, energy is being applied toward what you are thinking about. Your focus on the facts should tell you that you need to stay in today, and not distribute precious energy to nonexistent periods of time.

➤ Next, there is emotional energy. When your emotions become involved, energy is distributed to address what you are feeling. Emotional energy is used faster and with more intensity than any other form of energy in the body.

➤ Finally, there is spiritual energy. This type of energy connects to the core of your existence. It's where pure love is found, as you will see in Chapter 33.

As you are navigating back and forth between past events that have caused conflict and anxiety, and worrisome future events that have not yet arrived, you are using energy resources that can be more efficiently used today. Worry, conflict, anxiety, anger, and fear, all heighten your emotions, which misdirects your energy to what is not occurring in today; the time frame where they are most needed.

You must learn to focus your energy where it can best be utilized best: in the present. Staying in today, and maximizing your energy distribution there, can have a profound positive effect on your internal balance, and the healthy person you are trying to be.

 **TIME TO TAKE ACTION**

1. To stop the backward/forward principle from seriously affecting your life, keep your energies focused on the day you are living in. Start by consciously refusing to think about stressful past events. Self-coaching works here, too.

2. Take a good look at a future event you are worrying about. If you cannot do anything to alter its course, don't waste your energy thinking about it; that's where the anxiety comes from. Journaling about it, and how it makes you feel might help. Here's a rule to live by: If you can do something about future events, then do it. If not, stop worrying about it. Call it the *do or don't strategy*.

3. Don't allow others to influence the management of your time. You can listen to what they have to say, but make the decision about what you need to do, one that keeps your energies focused on what you need to do today. Maintain control over your boundaries.

4. Since energy distribution is so important, proportion yours in accordance with what you can realistically do today. Today demands energy to be supplied for you physically, intellectually, emotionally, and spiritually. Keep it about today.

5. Keep it conscious. The backward/forward principle and autopilot living go hand in hand. So, apply conscious thought as you are making decisions about where to use your energy.

 ## DRIVING IT HOME

You can always make a choice about what to focus on today. That's because it's happening right in front of you. If you focus your attention on today living, the influence of the energy thieves will be significantly reduced. That's life lived efficiently, and without all the backward/forward movement.

**YOUR MANTRA IS**: *I will stay in today; I will apply my energy in the here and now.*

 ## ONWARD

Journey living, in today, moment to moment, is the natural way to live life as we will see in our next chapter. Life does have a natural flow, and you need to learn to live in tune with it. I'm going to discuss life on life's terms next.

⬥⬥⬥⬥⬥⬥⬥⬥⬥⬥⬥⬥⬥

# CHAPTER 10

# Life on Life's Terms, and the Natural Flow

*Trying to force your will against life's natural progression only creates unnecessary pain. Try the natural flow, and run with nature's wind at your back.*

---

**PROCESSES TO EMPLOY:** Brutal Honesty, I Over E, Present/ Understand/Fix, Slowing Down Life's Pace, Fact-Finding, Journey Living, Keeping Life Simple, Life's Natural Flow, Life on Life's Terms, Slowing Down Life's Pace

---

IN NATURE, FLOW IS TYPICALLY DESCRIBED AS moving along or out steadily and continuously in a current or stream. When applied to human living, it is a state in which a person engaged in an activity is fully immersed in that activity, with all resources directed toward the successful conclusion of some specific goal. At the risk of going just a bit deep in our present discussion, and so that you can more fully understand the concepts associated with nature's natural flow, there are seven common laws which are thought to drive the universe. They are: The Principle of Mentalism, The Principle of Correspondence, The Principle of Vibration, The Principle of Polarity, The Principle of Rhythm, The Principle of Cause and Effect, and The Principle of Gender.

Without going into a full elucidation of these principles, suffice it to say that the universe, and for our purposes, nature, does subscribe to specific laws, and that we, as part of nature, are subject to those laws. Examples of natural laws are gravity, aerodynamics, oxygenation, pace, order (the arrangement or disposition of people or things in relation to each other according to a particular sequence), motion (for every action, there is an equal and opposite reaction), system rejuvenation (sleep), nutrition, causality (cause and effect relationships), and finally, evolution. Everything that happens in nature is subject to these natural laws, and nothing occurs in natural fashion that violates them. The closer our lives run in accordance to these natural laws, the more our lives coincide with nature, and as a result, the more connected and harmonious they will be. We are a living part of nature, and that fact will never change.

So, for the purposes of our discussion, I am defining living in tune with nature, that is, according to nature's natural flow, as: *living in accordance with nature's natural laws. It is our willingness to live true to the terms set by nature.*

Humans are constantly changing and evolving. Evolution is a natural process. It is subject to all the laws of nature, and works best when those laws are kept constant. Human beings, however, have been blessed with a spirit of free will, which turns on our "I want what I want" switch. It makes us think we are more powerful than we are, foolishly persuading us to challenge the laws of nature.

Free will can open the door for variety and new experiences in your life, but it also becomes the catalyst for both stress and conflict. If you stay close to nature's natural flows, you can still make life changes, while minimizing the damage along the way.

## My Way or the Highway

Free will can cause you to believe that you are entitled to some of those choices you are making, even when those choices challenge the laws of nature. We are all part of nature, subject to its laws, and we are at our best when what we are doing is consistent with the course nature sets. Nothing you choose to do can go against nature's flow, and not be difficult for you, or cause you unnecessary conflict and discomfort.

As a species, we often boast about challenging nature, and overcoming the obstacles it sets in our paths. We like to think that our boundaries are limitless, and that when we put our minds to it, there isn't anything we can't do. To some extent, it's good to challenge your limitations. Doing so allows you to gain a better understanding of your own personal capabilities. It also helps you set new directions for your life, and is instrumental in helping you achieve the goals you set for yourself.

It's nice to have things your own way. Unfortunately, this way of thinking can cause you to tenaciously invest your energies in situations that have you pitting yourself against life's natural flow, and making choices that aren't always good for you. Running against the wind can become your normal way of doing things, but watch your arrogance. Nature often has other ideas.

## Homeostasis, and the Pendulum Matrix

An interesting way to look at life is how it exists on a kind of human pendulum. A pendulum is a weight hung from a fixed point, so it can freely swing back and forth. The weight moves from side to side with the amount of the swing depending on the amount of force applied to it. We can look at human life as existing on a pendulum. When the pendulum is relaxed, that is when it's at the bottom, it represents homeostasis, which is the human organism existing in a balanced state. For our purposes, our balance is, of course, our physical, intellectual, emotional, and spiritual attributes.

If you give the pendulum a push, it moves to one side or the other. At that point, it is no longer relaxed, and becomes imbalanced. There's nothing wrong with your life pendulum being temporary out of balance as you stretch limitations, attempting to introduce new directions into your life. The trick is to have an adequate plan that allows the pendulum, that is your internal attributes, to return to a balance state. Unfortunately, we like to keep that pendulum moving as far in the direction of our choice as we can. We can be insatiable that way, which can lead to some interesting problems.

## Orville, Wilber, and the Natural Laws

I'm going to define a "natural law" as *an ordinance; a rule that derives from nature, and is binding on the actions of human beings.* Keep in mind that there is a difference between growing and expanding in tune with nature, and attempting to grow and expand in a way that is not natural for us. The following example illustrates this difference:

Man has long experimented with the concept of flying, and in developing that ability, many people lost their lives. Those who did used contraptions that were too heavy, too large, or not aerodynamically sound. Since these attempts violated natural laws, disaster was inevitable. At the turn of the twentieth century, Orville and Wilbur Wright built the world's first successful flying machine by addressing the natural laws of aerodynamics. Today, with advances in engineering and aerospace science, flying has become commonplace.

Granted, there are periods of trial and error before you can make a new invention work, but even in those trials, if you program the natural flow into your process, you should see more success, with less conflict, and less pain. If you take the time to develop your knowledge and understanding regarding what it would take to accomplish a dream, and systematically eliminate the parameters that are not naturally sound, you can achieve your goal with minimum discomfort, and with sustained success.

When you see what you want, rush to get it as fast as you can, and fail to consider life's natural flow, things can go sideways quickly. Violating life's natural flows causes you to experience the difficulties that come with your abbreviated and rebellious process. There is a danger of becoming a little-picture thinker, hell-bent on having things the way you want them, with no regard for the bigger picture, and the natural flow of your life. It is imperative that you become proficient at assessing the information that will allow you to see the big picture in any situation.

Many of us, all too often, see something; we want it, and we quickly go after it. Nothing in nature operates like that. Nature is deliberate, always functioning according to a specific plan. It operates according to the bigger picture, and it neither forgets that, nor lets us forget it. In fact, it demands that we understand and incorporate big-picture thinking into our plans. It will be much easier for us achieve our goals if we synchronize our methodologies with nature's flow. We can still arrive at our goals, but we just might need the aspirin a little less often.

## Nature as an Ally—
## Present/Understood/Fix; Au Naturel

When you use the present/understand/fix formula to assist you as you follow nature's natural flow, you are presenting your initial concern, followed by an in-depth attempt to understand all the facts honestly, and with as little emotion as possible. Then you devise your plan to fix the problem. I'll use an example to illustrate this:

You're a person with a typically high energy level. Lately however, it's been difficult to get up in the morning. You're also noticing that your energy level throughout the day isn't what it used to be. You started taking more vitamins, and you're eating better. Things should be changing, but they're not. So, what do you do? Your first order of business is to *present* the problem; you're tired and your energy level is down. Next, you would gather information; all those natural facts you need to *understand* the situation.

You decide that would be a good idea to review your entire daily routine. This information tells you that everything is on course until the evening hours. Recently, you decided to accept two hours of overtime to make a little more money. In addition, you increased the intensity of your evening workout. Also, as a way to relax, you're meeting some friends at night for a few drinks. In addition to intensifying your daily schedule, you're losing an hour of sleep every night.

So, a review of the information tells you that you were overdoing it, adding some alcohol, and losing some sleep. Obviously, none of this is in tune with nature's natural flow, and you're paying the price. It's time for a schedule change to *fix* the problem. You could have made the changes, but you might have avoided the exhaustion by staying a little closer to those natural laws.

Working with nature's natural flow has four advantages:

1. It allows you to slow down enough to use your mind on a far more efficient level than you do when you are in a rush.

2. It allows you to examine the information to determine if your plan is realistic and reachable.

3. It keeps you in sync with the natural order of things.

4. It allows you the time to incorporate temporary pauses, reassess your information, and apply any new approaches that may be more efficient.

## Nature, the Processes, and the Balance

Nature's natural flow applies to the way you function physically, intellectually, emotionally, and spiritually. Your life is governed by these laws and it's important that you stay in tune with natures natural flow to maintain your internal balance. Here's how:

1. Physically, you take care of your body. You stay away from anything that alters the way your body should function naturally.

2. Intellectually, you take the time to gather the facts without agendas and preconceived notions. Stay brutally honest and factual.

3. Emotionally, try to keep the pace of your life slow, and respond appropriately to information based on facts. Flip back to the 7 Practical Steps to Reduce Your Emotions in Chapter 4 for help.

4. Spiritually, you provide your spirit time and energy to connect with the more tranquil parts of your being (prayer and meditation).

How do you know if what you are planning to do violates nature's natural flow? You are going to feel:

➤ Physical strain                    ➤ Emotional anxiety

➤ Intellectual conflicts             ➤ Spiritual unrest

Working with nature's natural flow leads to attribute balance and system harmony. You may challenge nature. You may believe that the battle is worth waging and that somehow, you can go against nature's natural flow and win. Nature, however, doesn't forget, and nature's natural flow, the really big picture, is to reestablish itself when its flow is violated. So, if you swim against the river's mighty current once and win, you might want to continue the process. Somewhere along the line, however, expect nature to reestablish itself, and it will. It might be a good idea to learn how to hold your breath.

 **TIME TO TAKE ACTION**

1. Slow down enough to spend some time gathering the information that applies to something you wish to do. For example, if you want to learn how to skydive, talk to people, watch videos, read about it, and take skydiving lessons.

2. If you begin to feel conflict or anxiety as you attempt to secure what you want, it may be a red flag that you're working against the natural order of things. Rethink your position. You might identify a better approach.

3. Try not to make running against the wind your own natural flow. Research what you want to do, and make your decision based upon viable and realistic information. You can only run against the wind so long before nature blows back.

4. Running against nature's natural laws is often motivated by feelings of arrogance, pride, and entitlement. Emotions are always going to be part of the picture. Remember, use your intellect first. Get the facts, and, express your emotions based on intelligent information.

 ## DRIVING IT HOME

In the end, we are natural beings, and we are all subject to living in this natural world. As such, we are subject to its natural laws. When you learn to truly understand nature's natural flow, you can have all you need, and much of what you want, with the added luxury of avoiding nature's natural payback. It's much easier to be happy when you and nature are flowing in the same direction. Try the natural flow, and run with nature's wind at your back.

**YOUR DECLARATION IS:** *I'll go with the flow—easy and slow.*

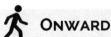 ## ONWARD

Those safe and unchallenged comfort zones of ours are such wonderful places to be, but sometimes, they can cause us to become stagnated and unchallenged. I'll be discussing comfort zones and the movement into growth next, as you learn how to include change in your process game plan.

◇◇◇◇◇◇◇◇◇◇◇◇◇

# CHAPTER 11

# Change, and the Route to Growth

*Change is the vehicle that leads to the sustained comfort you seek. Embrace it, and see your world come alive!*

---

**PROCESSES TO EMPLOY:** Brutal Honesty, I Over E, Present/ Understand/Fix, Slowing Down Life's Pace, Learning to Be Comfortable with Being Uncomfortable, Risk-Taking, Trust

---

WE ALL LIKE TO RELAX, AND WE all like to be comfortable. The human body routinely needs downtime. This helps us escape from our daily pressures, and gives us an opportunity to recharge and reload. Sometimes, those comfort zones work to our advantage. Relaxing to read a good book, meditating, taking a walk, engaging in a hobby, and enjoying a good movie are all examples of doing something that is pleasurable, but doesn't cause problems for us.

Many of us, however, have comfort zones that routinely lead to dysfunctional thoughts and behaviors, and, in the long run, can cause us pain and suffering. Changing our unhealthy routines can be challenging. I'm going to show you an efficient way to program healthy downtime into your life; one that can help you recharge and escape from life's pressure points, without causing problems for you.

## Comfortably Numb—Too Much of a Good Thing

The traditional definition of a "comfort zone" is a personal place or situation where one can feel at ease and without stress. As long as you stay within its parameters, a good comfort zone can work for you. However, human beings can be insatiable. We tend to indulge ourselves to the point that our behavior can become toxic, or at the very least, its overuse can create problems for us. The misuse of a comfort zone can lead to problematic routines that can seriously affect the quality of your life.

Overusing a comfort zone starts when you find something that feels good. You like that feeling, so you continue to engage in that comforting behavior. As time goes on, and your enjoyment in the comfortable behavior increases, you find ways to spend more time there. It may have started with an innocent hour watching your favorite television program, but now you are spending several hours in front of the television, with repeated visits to the kitchen for something to snack on.

The offshoot of your overused comfort zone is that you are neglecting some chores around the house, not adding much to your life intellectually, and you're gaining weight. What began as a simple way to reduce stress became something that began to work against you, and has created some new problems. It has become a rut, and it's time for change.

## Embracing the "Change Monster"

Change can make you feel uncomfortable. That uncomfortable feeling, however, is exactly what leads to inner growth, and to a lasting comfortable way of life. Becoming uncomfortable is actually a healthy component of growth-oriented change, and learning to become comfortable with this uncomfortable period of time is an essential part of change. To be comfortable with being uncomfortable seems contradictory. So, why in the world would you make a conscious decision to be uncomfortable? Here's an illustration:

Let's say you're fifty pounds overweight. You've tried numerous diets, both fad and legitimate. They all work for a while, but soon you're back to your old tricks, and here comes the weight. The reason you're having a difficult time is that the program you committed yourself to includes emotional deprivation and lots of work, making you feel uncomfortable. If you're going to have any chance to make your new eating plan have extended value, you're going to have to come to terms with being uncomfortable as you change the way you eat. This is what getting comfortable with being uncomfortable means. You will be uncomfortable until you adjust to the new way of eating, and that adjustment takes time, but have no worries. Your brain is equipped with a process called *habit formation*. This simply means that it has the ability to move through uncomfortable life situations, and redefine them as new comfort zones. So the uncomfortable time is temporarily uncomfortable until you give it time to become part of you. I'll be explaining how the processes become a living part of you in Chapter 29.

If you are going to stay uncomfortable, it would be understandable for you to have a problem with the approach. Your goal is to make the changes permanent, but before you do, you will be uncomfortable until you adjust to doing things differently. Change always has an uncomfortable component in its design. Be willing to stay committed through this temporary time in your plan though, because it creates the permanent change that will become the dramatic new you.

## No Pain, No Gain

There is unlimited knowledge hidden in the process of being comfortable with being temporarily uncomfortable. Learning about yourself lives there. This is where you test yourself, and define the strengths you never thought you had. Anyone who wants to be successful must push past their perceived limitations, and understand that the uncomfortable time during the acquisition process (the transition period) is temporary, and is exactly what leads to sustained change and happiness.

The uncomfortable time is your brain learning to understand and embrace your new life. Thus, it is an essential part of the growth process. Without it, the chances for permanent change are drastically reduced. There are two reasons that getting comfortable with being uncomfortable is so important:

1. It paves the way for success, which results from the discipline learned during the uncomfortable process of change associated with achieving your goal.

2. You will be presented with new information about yourself, information that stretches you through your current comfort zones, into uncomfortable territory, and beyond, into a new and more fulfilling life; to a new more comfortable you.

A new person is being created. This new person has capabilities the old comfortable version never dreamed of. Be that person!

## Getting Started

1. A good way to start this comfortable to uncomfortable to comfortable process is with some simple practice sessions. Pick something that will cause you to experience a small amount of discomfort. Physical exercise, if you're capable of this, is a good example, but you can apply the approach to anything you want to change. Start with a simple program, like five sit-ups, two push-ups, and maybe a half a minute of jumping jacks. Done in succession, they will quickly pull you from your comfort zone. Walking on a treadmill for five minutes might do the same thing for you. Keep doing this even though it's uncomfortable. Start slow. Above all, stay focused on your plan, and don't quit.

2. The next step is to increase the duration of your discomfort. Few goals are accomplished quickly, so understand that you are going to be doing this for a while. Don't rush! Increase your duration slowly, so the discomfort won't discourage you. You'll begin to understand the process your body, your mind, and your emotions are undertaking, and this will help you stick with your plan. Slow and committed builds confidence.

3. Stop thinking about your new temporary discomfort. That's negative energy. You don't want that. Focus on your goal. That's positive. Never move your concentration away from that.

4. Don't get ahead of yourself. Know what part of the plan you are doing today, and focus on that. Stay in the moment. It's those moments, all strung together, that produce success.

This is where it's important to take a good, honest look at yourself and decide how important being happy and fulfilled is to you. The level of happiness you realize will be equal to the amount of temporary discomfort you are willing to experience. Your clever and sophisticated brain will not only adjust to your temporary discomfort, it will begin to create a new and better comfortable way of living for you while you are temporarily uncomfortable. Yeah, you have that much control. You are powerful—if you want to be.

 ## TIME TO TAKE ACTION

1. Design your comfort zones with a plan that allows you to be in them for a temporary period of time, followed by a time to return to productive living.

2. Consciously set aside selected periods of time to engage in your comfort zones. Make those periods relatively short, and have a plan regarding how you will return to your responsibilities. You can write them in a planner, or use an app to keep track of them.

3. Change always has some discomfort associated with it. Don't be afraid to move outside your comfort zone. The better part of you lives there.

4. Your temporary uncomfortable zone is the gift that can change your world. Stay committed. Be happy with small movements forward. There is growth even in the little steps. The gains will come.

5. All growth is a process. Be willing to stretch beyond your perceived limits. That can be uncomfortable; however, keep in mind that you will come through this, and that your new comfort zone will be one that is happier than its predecessor. Go slow!

6. Never focus on your perceptions of your discomfort during a growth period. Focus your energies on achieving the goal you're aiming at. Stay focused, in today, and in the moment. Be determined.

7. Remove the idea of quitting from your world. The new way of life is to persevere. That's where winning lives.

 ## DRIVING IT HOME

Change isn't always comfortable, especially when you are stretching past your limitations and comfort zones to redefine who you are. While you're getting comfortable with being uncomfortable, mark and enhance your change moments. Make them feel good. It will take time, but you are worth the time it takes to get there, and you are worth that wonderful new life.

**YOUR DECLARATION IS**: *I will never quit; I will persevere, and I will create my new life!*

 ## ONWARD

Guilt and shame are process-growth killers. In the next chapter, I'm going to show you how emotional baggage from the past can affect your life, and you're going to see how forgiveness can empower you to move past it.

◇◇◇◇◇◇◇◇◇◇◇◇◇◇◇

# CHAPTER 12

# Redefining Life Through Forgiveness

*The choice to forgive sets the stage for the course your life will take, and defines your ability to love yourself, and others.*

---

**PROCESSES TO EMPLOY:** Brutal Honesty, I Over E, Present/ Understand/Fix, Slowing Down Life's Pace, Dignity, Forgiveness, Honor, Humility, Internal Focus, Settling Past Issues

---

WE ALL MAKE MISTAKES, AND WE ALL can have difficulty moving past them. The deep, abiding sense of guilt and shame we may feel for something we did can make it difficult to leave our past behind. Such feelings can make growth and happiness elusive. Moving past these times is essential. In this chapter, I'm exploring the life-changing power of forgiveness, and how you can apply it as a dynamic process in your life.

## It Begins

The moment you do something wrong, your spirit has been damaged, and the way you think and feel has been affected. You can shroud your thoughts and feelings about what you did with all kinds of defenses and avoidance tactics. None of them, however, will successfully leave the event in the past. You can also try to say that it's done, and in the past. It may be, but its emotional residue can affect you today.

As soon as you understand that you have done something that makes you feel guilt or shame, the process of forgiving yourself must begin. You need to take steps to successfully move yourself away from your mistake so that it no longer hurts you. When those steps are taken, the event can successfully be placed in the past, so it stops affecting the rest of your life. The Process Way of Life's path to forgiveness reduces the power of the event over you, and empowers you to be free of its effects permanently.

## Nothing to Be Ashamed Of

In its truest sense, forgiveness is nothing more than an admission of your humanity. It tells you that you made a mistake, and that you don't have to carry the pain it has caused forever. When it is addressed, you can be whole and happy again. In the more traditional mode of thought, "forgiveness" is described as a state of pardon, of absolution, exoneration, and mercy. Notice, however, that these are all the result of forgiveness. For you to realize true forgiveness, there must be a process to make this happen.

To begin this discussion, I offer a different definition of "forgiveness" as it applies to the Process Way of Life. *Forgiveness is the result of a step-by-step understanding and systematic removal of negative energy and self-defeating thoughts, with a plan to ensure that the wrongdoing won't happen again.* Forgiveness is a process that can restore you to intellectual and emotional sanity, and ultimately support internal balance.

Say you have done something that you believe is significant enough to have caused pain to someone else, and this has damaged your feelings about yourself. You may be having a difficult time letting the event go, and are unable to move past it. The "sticking spot" regarding what has occurred can present itself in three ways:

1. It can cause you to feel sad and experience guilt and shame.

2. You can intellectualize it, deny it, and use your defenses to make yourself feel better. (I'll be discussing defenses in Chapter 14.)

3. You can begin to either consciously or unconsciously punish yourself for what you have done, since you feel that you deserve sanctions that are commensurate with the seriousness of the deed.

Since none of these can bring you to absolution, they cannot prepare you to reestablish growth and personal happiness. That's because none of them are addressing the central issue: facing what you have done, and forgiving yourself.

Regardless of whether you admit or deny that you have done something wrong, the event creates negative energy. The facts are the facts, and nothing changes the facts. If you have done something wrong, then that is what you did. You can't change it by rationalizing it, dismissing it, intellectualizing it, or blaming someone else.

If your commitment to growth is real, you acknowledge what you have done, own it, and begin the process of reconciling to others and to yourself. Owning what you have done, making amends, and establishing a route back to growth is essential, and is a process that you must hold yourself accountable to both embrace and accomplish. Without doing so, forgiving yourself cannot occur, and you do not want to incorporate this unaddressed situation, and the toxins that accompany it, as part of your movement forward.

## The Basic Plan

The features of the Process Way of Life's plan to address accountability, and subsequently, your ability to forgive yourself are:

➤ You must first understand that there is negative energy attached to what you have done. That damage could be to yourself only, or there may be others involved.

➤ You need to summon some old friends to help you. Here, you call upon brutal honesty, I Over E, and slowing down life's pace (see Chapters 2, 3, and 4). Your first order of business is to be factual and honest in your representation of what has happened. There are no excuses and no extenuating circumstances.

➤ Make a list of everyone who may have been affected by your actions. Then, be responsible enough, humble enough, and brave enough to make amends with those people. This may include expressions of sorrow, and you need to make a concerted effort to understand what your actions caused them to experience. It may also include what you may need to do to help repair the damage caused by your actions.

➤ You need to consider the dynamics of your own thoughts and emotions and how they led you to behave as you did. This is extremely important so that you can understand not only what you did, but why you did it, and how to avoid doing it again.

Considering these points, here's the *Process Way of Life plan to forgive yourself*—by the numbers:

1. Be honest with yourself, and admit what you have done.

2. Be willing to put the feelings of the other person before your own.

3. Get all the facts, especially, from the person you may have hurt.

4. Be willing to listen to what they have to say, without judgment or self-protection.

5. Be willing to make amends for what you have done by addressing all of their concerns.

6. Go slow enough to make sure that you are not missing anything important.

7. Think about how and why you did what you did. Understand your motivations.

8. Formulate a plan to help ensure that it doesn't happen again.

9. Carry out that plan.

You will need to be humble enough to get past your arrogance and defenses. I'm discussing humility in Chapter 28. If you need help with the plan, talk to someone.

When your plan is in place, you need to commit yourself to addressing *all of it,* so that you may set the stage for your continued movement forward. Doing so helps remove negative energy from your movement forward. Being healthy is all about positive forward energy.

Forgiving yourself is a process approach that is essential to remove guilt and shame, hold you accountable as you attempt to assist others whom you have hurt, and help ensure that the event doesn't happen again. If even one part of the plan is avoided, the potential for internal recovery becomes reduced, and you can expect a level of growth and movement forward that may be significantly compromised. Life has no still waters, and an unreconciled past always moves forward.

As for the people whose lives you may have affected, don't forget that these people have feelings, and they may feel pain and conflict as a result of your actions. Make a sincere and heartfelt attempt to help them reestablish peace and sanity in their lives. You took something from them, and you must do all you can to make amends and help them restore what was taken, regardless of how insignificant it may seem to you.

### Forgiveness—in Reverse

What can you do if you are carrying baggage which comes from others who have hurt you? The negative energy that you carry forward from not forgiving someone else can also sabotage your life journey. These people hurt you, took something from you, made you angry, and have caused you to feel conflict and pain.

The most important rule to remember about forgiveness is that you really can't forgive anyone else until you forgive yourself. That's why I am presenting this at the end of the chapter. Assuming that you are willing to take the Process Way of Life steps to forgive yourself, you can prepare yourself to forgive someone else.

The most pronounced obstacle in your way will be our own anger. Few people want to forgive their offenders, especially when those people don't seem remorseful. Anger quickly gets in the way, and most people would rather pay the offender back, in kind. That is exactly what the negative energy is all about. It's also the first thing you have to let go. I'm discussing how to define anger, and what to do with it in Chapter 18. This will help you move past their deed.

Forgiving them is also going to require humility. The antithesis of the arrogance that anger can create, humility moves slower, and helps you to stay grounded so that you may more efficiently work with your feelings. If you feel that you can or must confront someone who made you angry, it's important to do so under the right circumstances. Chapter 16 discusses how to Confront Others Peacefully. You'll need to incorporate anger reduction, humility, and peaceful confrontation into your plan.

My last piece of advice, especially if you're holding on to anger and don't feel that you can let go of it, is to seek the advice of someone close. Counselors are quite capable of helping you move through the anger that will help you to let go of the past, formulate a plan to forgive your offender, and relieve yourself of the negative energy which can continue to hurt you. If you are having a difficult time forgiving someone who has hurt you, love yourself enough to get help.

 **TIME TO TAKE ACTION**

1. Acknowledge that you made a mistake, and that it must be addressed so that it does not continue to move forward with you.

2. Be brutally honest as you piece together what occurred. Focus on the facts. Go slow.

3. With the facts in order, create a plan to help you avoid any reoccurrences in the future. Execute each and every component of your plan to the best of your abilities. It can be difficult, and you may want to try to fix it quickly, but go slow, so you don't miss anything. You don't want any negative energy moving forward with you.

4. If any part of this plan is difficult for you, it makes good sense to talk it over with someone. This could be someone you trust, your spouse or partner, or if necessary, a counselor. Be humble.

5. Make amends to anyone who has fallen victim to what you have done, except when to do so would injure them or others. It's difficult to forgive yourself if you have victims who are still hurting. Hold yourself accountable on this one. Help them to feel better about what happened.

6. Forgive yourself before you try to forgive someone else. If you can't forgive someone who hurt you, get help. Don't allow the negative energy from this to become part of who you are.

You can't lie, you can't be arrogant or prideful, and you can't run away. Face the process of forgiveness head-on with a well-defined plan to help the people you may have hurt, and yourself. Use the plan outline I presented earlier as a template for the steps you need to take.

 **DRIVING IT HOME**

When you ruminate over negative thoughts and experiences, you give life to the past and it continues to exert its influence in the present. Negative energy is a lightning rod to self-destruction. Intellectual, emotional, and spiritual freedom are the magnificent byproducts of process-generated personal forgiveness. Remember, forgiveness is all about the three H's: honesty, humility, and help.

**YOUR DECLARATION IS:** *I will forgive myself and others completely, I will live free.*

 **ONWARD**

Little in life has such a profound effect on us as fear. It can be one of life's most debilitating antagonizers. Next, I'm going to take a close look at this devitalizing nemesis, and help you reduce its impact on your life, and your internal balance.

◇◇◇◇◇◇◇◇◇◇◇◇◇

# CHAPTER 13

# The Fear Factor

*Fear can cause emotional and intellectual paralysis. Challenge yourself with something you think you could never do, and you'll find that you can overcome almost anything.*

**PROCESSES TO EMPLOY:** Brutal Honesty, I Over E, Present/ Understand/Fix, Slowing Down Life's Pace, Fact-Finding, Living in the Moment, One-Day-at-a-Time, Risk-Taking, Settling Past Issues, Trust

FEAR IS ONE OF THE MOST EFFICIENT happiness killers in the world. Nothing can cause you to feel physically, intellectually, emotionally, and spiritually incapacitated more than fear. All of us experience it. It's important to understand how it attacks you, and what you can do about it.

Fear is a chain reaction in the brain that starts with some kind of stressful event. It triggers the release of chemicals that can cause you to experience physical reactions like a racing heart, accelerated breathing, and energized muscles. Fear instigates the onset of the fight-or-flight response: the split-second decision to fight your way out of a threat or run away as fast as you can. The stimulus could be a spider, the big test, a needle, or even a sudden loud noise.

Your goal in this chapter is to gain an understanding of what fear is, and how to address it. This will help you to move past the problems it causes.

## The Rational and the Irrational

I am dividing fear into two categories: rational fears and irrational fears. Rational fears are fears that come from real circumstances. They represent events that can have moderate to serious implications. Irrational fears don't always come from real circumstances. Often, what the person fears will not come to pass, or at least not with the intensity they imagined it would.

"Fear value" measures the intensity of what you are feeling when you are afraid of something. Irrational fears tend to have more fear value than rational fears since their origin, and often the course they will take, are not defined. A fearful event could be assigned a minor, moderate, or intense value, depending on how it makes you feel. The higher the fear value, the less control you feel you have.

When what is feared is real, we tend to assign a fear value that more closely corresponds to what we are experiencing. That's because we understand the situation better, and we can be more realistic regarding what it can do to us, and how we can address it.

Irrational fears, however, though they may stem from real-life circumstances, often develop into overdone emotional productions. We firmly believe that they have powers that they simply cannot have. There is no rational explanation for the level of fear they cause, so we begin to imagine what could happen. This makes us that much more afraid, increasing the fear value even more.

Rational fears tend to be more accurately addressed by our conscious thoughts. You can think about them, try to understand them, and hopefully, do something about them. Irrational fears are more automatic. Something happens or maybe you begin to think about something, and automatically you feel the fear. You become tense, have difficulty focusing, and you may start to obsess about what you think might happen.

Fears can cause dramatic changes in your life. They change the way you think, robbing you of some of the control you need to function efficiently. Also, since you do understand that you are afraid, and as a result, are operating with less control in your life, you tend to think about yourself in negative ways. Being afraid can put you in an "I can't" position, which causes you to place limitations on your abilities. You can feel victimized. You can begin to think about yourself in ways that can hurt you. You may feel ashamed, guarded, and defensive about it. You may also become more judgmental toward others. Fear can also cause discrimination, isolation, and poor judgment.

You will never alleviate fear. It is a basic human emotion. It serves to notify you that something can be threatening or dangerous to you. However, since fear can attach itself to your emotions and become irrational, the goal is to confront it before it becomes strong enough to have a negative impact on your life.

## The Faces of Fear

Examining the faces of fear will help you understand the role that it plays in your life, and some of the methods you may be using to cope with it. Fear causes you to go "into character." When you're in character, you often follow a script that causes you to address your fear inappropriately, or to avoid it altogether.

### The Safe Face

Our first face of fear is our *safe face*. Here, we are overly cautious. We may overtly verbalize our fear. For example, we may be afraid of heights, roller coasters, or insects. Sometimes, we will attempt to face something that frightens us, but we will minimize our involvement in the situation. We may bring ourselves close to the threatening situation, but never fully involve ourselves in the activity. Our safe face could be addressing a fear that is rational, or it could be irrational. Since we are avoiding the fear, we know it exists. It is a conscious fear.

When a fear is conscious, and you understand that it's there, the potential to define it is enhanced, and we can take some steps to address it. As a result, cautious fear has a higher potential of being resolved. Our safe face is attempting to face the fear, and we are doing so with the level of moderation that can bring us close to resolution if we're willing to take a few extra steps.

### The Victim Face

Our second face of fear is our *victim face*. Here, the strategy is to surrender to the fear, never make a real attempt to change it, and always do our best to avoid it. In the short term, it feels as though this is a successful way to deal with the fear, because we rarely come face-to-face with it. Unfortunately, we never change it either. The victim face keeps us in a victim frame of mind, often in a subordinate position, and we are rarely looking for a way out of the fear response. Anytime we surrender to something or someone that keeps us in a victimized frame of mind, we are allowing ourselves to become prisoners of the fear. We should never be surrendering ourselves to our fears. There are always ways to address them.

### The Paranoid Face

Our third face of fear is our *paranoid face*. Here, we may assume that horrible things are going to happen, and we tend to emotionally react in a fashion that is not only unrealistic, but usually overdone. An example is the fear of the dark—you know, monsters? We will see the fear as greater than it is, and we will see it infused into situations of our lives where not only does it not belong, but it probably doesn't exist there either.

Though paranoid fear is also expressed on a conscious level, it's more difficult to address than safe fear, because such a large percentage of its dynamics are emotional and unrealistic. Before we begin to reduce paranoid fear, we need to take steps to define its "real fear value" so that we may understand it. Then we can take steps to address it. We can do this by soliciting the help of others. There, we can discuss the fear, put it in a more realistic perspective, and begin to devise some ways to move past it.

### The Attack Face

The last face of fear is our *attack face*. This is, by far, the most insidious of our fear faces. The attack face does not allow its actors to understand that they are in character. Instead of showing fear, those who use the attack face become aggressive, and apply that aggression in situations where it doesn't belong. They may quickly establish boundaries, are often over-opinionated, and unrelenting as they continue to express their opinions. They tend to discriminate, and draw boundaries where boundaries don't need to exist. They are often "in-your-face," stubborn, and close-minded.

Our attack-faced friends, unlike all the other faces we are examining, rarely, if ever, remove the mask, and use it as a survival device that is never turned off. It is the type of fear that is most difficult to understand, and most resistant to change. People using the attack face like what they are doing, feel a false sense of power, and steadfastly combat external efforts to help them understand their fear face as a scripted role. The fear face also hurts more family members and friends than any of the other fear faces.

Before you can reduce any fear, it's important to reduce its fear value. Here are the important steps you can take to make that happen.

## REDUCING FEAR VALUE—THE 7 STEPS

| The Advice | How to Make It Happen |
|---|---|
| Stay in the moment. | Fear usually comes from something in your past, and/or something you're anticipating. Use my suggestions from Chapter 8. |
| Slow down your breathing. | Remember, our breathing exercises from Chapter 5; meditate if you must. |
| Take a break. | Remove yourself from the situation if you can. Give yourself a chance to think. |
| Gather the facts. | Use I Over E. Talk to others, if necessary. |
| Define and mark positive territory. | Use the techniques I set down in Chapter 3. |
| Get out of your own head. | Talk your fears over with someone. This helps you work with the facts. |
| Make a plan to face your fear. | A step-by-step plan helps here. Get someone to help you: friends, family, a counselor, etc. |

As you can see, this debilitating nemesis has many faces. They are nothing more than your mind's attempts to deal with fear. It's all about reducing fear value. The fear value will be reduced, if you are willing to take the steps necessary to address it. Try to face your fears head on. Be willing to push past your limits, and get help if you need it. Never let your life gift take a backseat to fear.

 ## TIME TO TAKE ACTION

1. Be willing to look at yourself with brutal honesty, and start to define any fears that may be affecting your life.

2. Never attempt to hide or disguise a fear because you are afraid of what someone will think about you. Try to understand where your fear is coming from. Be willing to get help. There's nothing to be ashamed of.

3. Use the 7 Steps to Reduce Fear Value. Get help if you need it.

4. Sometimes, the fear can be addressed in a few easy steps. Sometimes, it takes a bit longer, and sometimes you will need some professional help. A counselor can help you put together a plan to reduce your fear.

5. Take a look at any anger you may be experiencing, especially if it occurs often. It may be your way to cover up some type of fear. Remember this: almost every form of anger has a component of fear associated with it. Get to the fear, and you might just see that you aren't so angry.

6. Remember that fear causes you to focus your energies on what has happened, and what might happen. This takes you out of the moment. To help avoid this, employ your processes. Use Present/Understand/Fix (Chapter 2), Brutal Honesty (Chapter 3), I Over E (Chapter 4), Slowing Down Life's Pace (Chapter 5), Living in the Moment (Chapter 8), and Staying in Today (Chapter 9).

 **DRIVING IT HOME**

Taking on your fear is a huge step. It's so important that you become a person who is willing to define and address your fears so that they don't cripple you. It's an incredible feeling full of empowering properties. Be that powerful person.

**YOUR DECLARATION IS**: *I will face my fears; I will feel my power.*

 **ONWARD**

Lies and defenses—they may look like they are protecting you, but in the end, they can lay waste to your best efforts to become the happy, fulfilled person you are working to be. I'll be addressing lies, defenses, and how truth cures in the next chapter.

# CHAPTER 14

# Lies, Defenses, and How Truth Cures

*There is no lie more damaging than the one you tell yourself.*
*It's a subtle and tragic form of abuse that you may never recover from.*

**PROCESSES TO EMPLOY:** Brutal Honesty, I Over E, Present/ Understand/Fix, Slowing Down Life's Pace, Fact-Finding, Internal Focus, Truth-Telling

SOUND INFORMATION IS AN IMPORTANT KEY to human survival. Since the human mind never stops processing information, working with the facts is imperative. The mind's primary function is to help us survive intellectually and emotionally. It can be creative and sensitive, but it can also be diabolical. It will use whatever resources are available to it to ensure its own survival, even if it means altering the presentation of its information to its unsuspecting owner.

Yes, our minds can lie to us. This misdirection of intellectual energy can occur at the slightest inkling of a potential threat to the system. It is the product of a mind that can reprogram resources that were meant for survival and internal comfort to a more sinister plan. Our brains have developed strategies that can alter the truth, and they are equipped with a sophisticated arsenal of complicated tools to carry out this task.

# The Best Defense Is a Strong Offense

Defenses, or defense mechanisms, as they are formally referred to, are the tools that your brain uses to help you survive in a world that can be a harsh place for you to live. Under normal circumstances, they are healthy tools that keep you in a state of intellectual and emotional balance. When you begin to misuse one or more of your defenses though, it can quickly move your internal stability into a state of imbalance, since they can misrepresent the facts. Here's a list of some of the more basic defense mechanisms:

➢ **DENIAL**—the refusal to accept reality or fact, acting as if a painful event, thought, or feeling did not exist.

➢ **PROJECTION**—the assigning of undesired thoughts, feelings, or impulses onto another person who does not possess them.

➢ **REPRESSION**—the unconscious blocking of unacceptable thoughts, feelings, and impulses.

➢ **INTELLECTUALIZATION**—making something sound more important than it is, or providing what seems like an intelligent reason for doing something.

➢ **RATIONALIZATION**—attempting to explain or justify one's behavior or attitude with logical, plausible reasons, even when these are not true or appropriate.

➢ **SUBLIMATION**—modifying the natural expression of an inappropriate behavior (especially a sexual one) to one that is socially acceptable.

➢ **COMPENSATION**—overachieving in one area to compensate for shortcomings in another.

➢ **DIVERSION**—attempting to move attention away from an event or behavior to something that has nothing to do with what is happening.

Let's look at an example of the way in which defense mechanisms operate:

## THE MARRIAGE ENCOUNTER

John and Mary have been married for five years. John comes from an emotionally stifled family. His father was an alcoholic, and his mother worked part-time to help with the bills. Emotional disclosure was not permitted in his home, and the environment was defensive and often angry. Though John does not drink, he displays some of the characteristics he learned during childhood. Mary earned her bachelor's degree in nursing. She is the charge nurse at a hospital and comes from a family that was open, warm, and very communicative.

John has difficulty when Mary corrects him, as gentle as she is. First, John says that he did not do what Mary said he did (denial). Then, John overemphasizes something good that he did (compensation). Finally, when challenged about the way he is behaving, John tries to make his decision look intelligent when it clearly is not (intellectualization). John's defenses will cause an argument between he and his wife, when all John had to do was admit that he could have done things differently. Mary had no intention of hurting John, who was quite positive that she was.

Emotionally, John couldn't accept the criticism as anything but an attack, so his defenses kept him from hearing the truth. John may have avoided the truth and protected himself from his perceived attacker, but he is now at odds with his spouse, and since he cannot admit his mistake, he is destined to repeat the behavior. An overused defense system can cause you to become resistive to change. When this happens, you may avoid those uncomfortable feelings that come with personal growth. These "growing pains" are an essential part of your healthy development.

# Fool's Gold

Many of us lie because we have fooled ourselves into believing that this strategy is more efficient, and will yield better results than telling the truth. We may also lie because, emotionally, we fear losing something. Others might see us as weaker than we want them to see us. So, the truth can be manipulated, a habit that, in the long run, can only complicate our lives, and cause problems for us.

As you learned in Chapter 2, we need truth to become secure with ourselves. Since lies present us with inaccurate information, they cause errors in judgment. The inaccurate information affects our feelings about ourselves and our relationships with others. The very strategy we thought would provide us with an advantage leaves us vulnerable and open to defeat. We lose the power that truth can create, and we find ourselves having difficulty understanding the difference between what is real, and what we have created.

When you lie, you are going to feel system imbalance.

- Intellectually, you will feel conflicted, since you know you are doing something wrong.

- Emotionally, you will feel discomfort, guilt, shame, fear, and/or insecurity.

- Physically, lies always initiate elevations in heart rate, breathing, and nervous system functions; adrenaline increases; eye contact shifts; you will feel less comfortable.

- Spiritually, you move away from the essence of who you are; you focus more on dishonest worldly strategies, and lose the connection to the center of your being.

Being honest with yourself is one of the most intrinsic and most important forms of honesty. Here are some basic rules to help you stay honest with yourself:

## The 7 Basic Rules of Honesty

1. Be humble, considerate, and open to others' opinions.

2. Identify the defense mechanisms you use.

3. Get your pride in check; be humble.

4. Never use a lie to manipulate another person.

5. When you lie or make a mistake, be willing to admit it.

6. Go slow, stay close to the facts, and work with your intellect.

7. Recognize truth as power, and a lie as the power-killer it is.

You can fool the world and yourself sometimes. You may even get away with it for a while. Eventually, however, the gig is up, and you are going to come back to yourself. It's difficult to feel growth when you're lying and defending your way through life. So it's important to stay with the truth, and identify any defenses you may be using. If you're lies and defenses have caused problems in your life, honesty and your forgiveness can help clear the slate as you learned in Chapter 12. Uncomplicate your life. Keep it honest.

 **TIME TO TAKE ACTION**

1. Know that if you are defending yourself, it's usually because you are insecure. Just focus on the facts. Be willing to present honest information. There's more security there.

2. Don't personalize what someone else says, and don't generalize it into a global attack on you. Doing do will instigate defenses quickly. Hear what they have to say.

3. Before you do anything, slow your life down enough to routinely think about what you're doing. Chapter 5 has the information to do this. Don't react quickly. Practice the art of applying thought before you react. Think, and then respond; honestly.

4. Knowing that the brain can be that diabolical trickster, sort through the information but do so with critical introspection.

Always address the possibility that what you're thinking may be wrong or, at least, needs to be refined just a bit.

5. Refer the information you are receiving back to the list of defenses mentioned earlier. See if you might be using any of them as a strategy that may alter the truth.

6. Misuse of defenses causes system imbalance. Review what's happening physically, intellectually, emotionally, and spiritually. If these changes are occurring, you're probably in a defensive posture. Slow down and reevaluate the situation. Know that you won't fall apart without your defenses. You'll just face the truth. Change starts there.

7. Here's that brutal honesty thing again. The truth may make you feel uncomfortable, but this will only last for a short time. Be willing to embrace the truth. You'll find peace and freedom there.

 ## DRIVING IT HOME

In all you do, it's important to understand that your body, mind, emotions, and spirit are all intimately linked. Lying can affect you on every level. The truth, however, empowers every measure of your existence. There's a fine line between using defenses for survival, and to keep you from facing the truth.

**YOUR DECLARATION IS:** *I will be less defensive; I will embrace the truth!*

 ## ONWARD

We all want to be happy, but what happens when we're not feeling so good about our lives, and others around us seem to be happy in theirs? In the next chapter, I'm going to look at envy, and what you can do to stop this self-esteem robber.

CHAPTER 15

◇◇◇◇◇◇◇◇◇◇◇◇◇

# The Enemy Within

*Envy is your mind's most efficient way of telling you that you don't measure up—to yourself.*

---

**PROCESSES TO EMPLOY:** Brutal Honesty, I Over E, Present/ Understand/Fix, Slowing Down Life's Pace, Goal-Setting, Internal Focus, Reduction of Destination Living, Truth-Telling

---

**WE EXIST IN A WORLD THAT RARELY,** if ever, is a fair and equitable place to live. We are taught that we are all supposed to be equal. However, when you look outside of yourself, you see others who seem to have more, and who, in your estimation, have you at a disadvantage. Their lives seem to be so much better than yours. There are so many reasons to arrive at the conclusion that you don't measure up.

All this comparing yourself to others and coming up short can cause you to become unsure about who you are, and what others may be thinking about you. When you look at yourself, something seems to be missing. When this happens, you can become envious of other people. As you continue in this self-demeaning process, it starts to become the way you routinely view your position in the world. Soon, you have lost sight of what you were envying. Now, envy has become the way you live life.

## A Look in the Mirror

I'm defining "envy" as *a feeling of discontent that occurs when you think you lack another's superior quality, achievement, or possession, and either desire it or wish that the other person didn't have it.* This can make you feel inferior, and you want to do something to make the uncomfortable feeling stop. Envy can occur when you think you are lacking in items like finances, good looks, possessions, position in the world, physical prowess, etc. This may be true, but even those who are wealthy, attractive, and successful can fall prey to envy.

Envy has little, if anything, to do with what another person has. Envy is really a self-esteem issue. It tends to live in the minds of those who think poorly of themselves. It can quickly put you at a disadvantage. Regardless of what you do, you never stack up well in comparison to your friends, and you never seem to feel good about what you do have, which is almost always more than you think.

Envy is an emotional issue. If you take the time to examine the situation clearly, you will see that it is quite fixable from the inside. This, however, is very difficult when you are focusing your attention outside of yourself, where the problem does not live. This is akin to hearing a disturbing noise inside your home which is coming from your furnace, and focusing your attention outside on your swimming pool as you attempt to fix it. It's important to work from the inside to make the noise stop. So it is with envy. Another's qualities and possessions are not the issue. You need to go inside yourself to find the problem.

## The Pain of It All

The society we live in tends to value looking good, being wealthy, having great careers, influence, power, and anything else that seems to add the glitter to our lives. When you don't have these, and others seem to, your envious disposition causes you to become disenchanted with yourself, and that old feeling of worthlessness sets in. You might even do your best to level the playing field by trying to draw negative attention to the other person. Spreading some rumor about them might work, or focusing on some negative trait could help. The real pain comes when you realize that all this outside focus hasn't changed one thing, and you are still miserable.

If you would simply look at yourself, you might just see that these negative feelings aren't about them. It's not "Well, if I could just have what they have, I'd be happy." It is about "If I focus on myself, gather the information to help me feel good about myself, establish my plan to get there, and execute my plan, I can become happy with myself."

Regardless of what you acquire on the outside, everything you think and feel is on the inside. All the glitter in the world won't fix what you're feeling. All too soon, the glitter vanishes, and what was shiny becomes pale. Feeling good on the inside, however, adds glitter to your external world. The reverse cannot happen. In the end, envy is nothing more than a red flag that signals that you are unhappy with yourself. The secret is not to medicate with external acquisitions, but to identify and address the internal insecurities that are producing the envy, and subsequently, your unhappiness.

## The 7 Traits of an Envious Person

1. You feel that others have more of something than you.

2. You attempt to "brag up" what you have or do.

3. You feel uncomfortable and insecure around others.

4. You are competitive to a fault.

5. You judge others for everything.

6. You become angry when others succeed.

7. You gossip about others.

Now compare the 7 traits of an envious person with the 7 traits of a secure person. This is what you should be working to achieve.

# The 7 Traits of a Secure Person

1. You are not concerned about what others have.

2. You are humble and quiet about what you have.

3. You feel comfortable and secure around others.

4. You enjoy competition, but don't always have to win.

5. You are accepting of others as they are.

6. You are happy to see others become successful.

7. You are always complimentary when you speak of others.

Realizing that you are feeling envious of someone can be a positive step in your life since it signals internal concerns, if you're willing to look at them. Stop looking outside yourself and focus on what is causing you to feel insecure and at a disadvantage internally. Then, you can make the changes that help you feel good about yourself, and reduce the instances of envy that are causing your pain. Remember, you have all you need to be happy on the inside. Change starts there. Do measure up—to yourself.

 **TIME TO TAKE ACTION**

1. Focus on who you are from the inside. Write down both your strengths and your weaknesses (aka, what you need to change). Work with the facts. It's I Over E here. Flip back to Chapter 4 if you need to refresh yourself. Identify what you need to change.

2. Stop comparing yourself with others. You can never know anyone else's whole story, and things might not be as wonderful as you think they are.

3. Know that if you focus your energies on making yourself who you want to be, and never give up, you can't fail. Focus on you, and follow your own dream.

4. Take some time to define exactly what will make you a happy person, on the inside. Write it down if you need to. Don't rely on material items or quick fixes. You'll be surprised to see just how much good is in there when you take the time to look.

5. While you're focusing on inside concerns, go easy on yourself. Concentrate on the positives, too. Focusing on your positive attributes, large or small, trains your brain to feel better about yourself. If you want to tear the envy house down, stop reinforcing it.

 ## DRIVING IT HOME

Envy is nothing more than slow suicide. The very moment you begin to envy another, your own life begins to die. Envy is not a look out to a world that is better than yours. It's a mirror. You are seeing yourself. Stop this self-esteem robber in its tracks.

**YOUR DECLARATION IS:** *I will envy no one; I will love myself.*

 ## ONWARD

All too often, you may find yourself having something you need to say, but you are afraid to let it out. In the next chapter, I'm going to examine the fear of confronting others, and what you can do to make it a much easier process.

◇◇◇◇◇◇◇◇◇◇◇◇◇

# CHAPTER 16

# Confronting Others Peacefully

## Avoiding the Up-and-Down Syndrome

*Confrontations should have little to do with agitated displays of anger and frustration. Express yourself with warmth, and pave the way for fruitful communicative discourses.*

---

**PROCESSES TO EMPLOY:** Present/Understand/Fix, Brutal Honesty, I Over E, Slowing Down Life's Pace, Conflict Resolution, Effective Communication, Humility, Listening, Risk-Taking, Warm Confrontation

---

IN OUR DAILY INTERACTIONS WITH OTHER PEOPLE, we have all found ourselves needing to express something that has upset or angered us. For some of us, expressing our concerns to others is relatively easy. For others, however, it can be a painstaking process involving intense emotions, followed by anger and frustration, and finally either an explosion or no action at all.

People who have a difficult time with confrontations find themselves overcome with anxiety and often lash out emotionally, and only after a period of angry rehearsal. By that time, they have lost sight not only of the focal point of the issue, but also how best to present it.

Confrontation can be problematic for two reasons:

1. We don't understand that we don't have to present our position with anger, and therefore the encounter does not have to be a verbal battle.

2. We spend too much time anticipating the response of the other person.

The assumption that anger will be present in a confrontation, and the fear of an angry response from the other person, often leads us to do absolutely nothing. It also leaves us with feelings of anger and frustration, and we are doomed to reexperience the unresolved event at some time in the future. To avoid a confrontation and still be able to move on with our lives, we convince ourselves that the matter has either been resolved or that it wasn't that important to begin with. This leaves us with the much sought-after feeling of relief, but not confronting the issue almost ensures that the behavior will be displayed again.

As expected, the issue that needs to be confronted reoccurs. Now, we become angry all over again. We go through all the same cognitive/emotional steps. We fight with ourselves to confront the situation, and once again, we back down and do nothing, only to reexperience the problem. This is something I call the *up-and-down syndrome*, which I define as:

1. the understanding that something or someone needs to be confronted (up),

2. the point where we convince ourselves that everything is fine, or that the matter cannot be resolved, and we do nothing (down),

3. the reoccurrence of the same issue once again.

It's a continuous up-down encore performance.

# Ghost Screaming

Sometimes the emotions that stem from not confronting someone can become so intense that we begin to talk to ourselves about the problem, with much emotion. I call this behavior *ghost screaming*. This is where we begin to have emotionally laden conversations with the person we aren't confronting. We begin by rehearsing what we want to say to the other person. Soon we are in a heated debate with someone who isn't there.

Ghost screaming is nothing more than a misguided attempt to organize the information in a situation with the hopes of bringing it to some type of conclusion. It's our way of trying to put closure on a situation that requires confronting another individual, without the confrontation.

Ghost screaming is an emotional outcry. This behavior occurs when we have become so frustrated with a person, or some situation, that we can't see our way out of it. We may anticipate that the other person will not cooperate, or that the situation, for whatever reason, is not fixable. The real explanation, however, is that we are afraid to confront the other person.

Most of us either run away from confrontations, or we create some quasi-intellectual explanation as to why confronting the situation won't work. In the end, however, the situation doesn't change, we continue to scream, and we are becoming frustrated, angry, and very unhappy with ourselves. It's important to understand if you are having difficulty with confrontations.

## 7 Signs That You Have Difficulty Confronting Others

1. You feel anxiety before you have to discuss something.

2. You have trouble organizing the facts about the situation.

3. You rehearse the "script" over and over again.

4. You are afraid of the other person's response.

5. You begin to have doubts about your point.

**6.** You look for ways to avoid the confrontation.

**7.** You begin to talk to them when they are not present.

If this is how you think and feel, you're probably having difficulty confronting others. There is hope though.

## 7 Ways to Help You Confront Others

**1.** Prepare what you want to say.

**2.** Stay close to the facts, and keep your emotions down.

**3.** Write the important points down.

**4.** Talk the matter over with someone you trust.

**5.** Decide the best time to confront the other person.

**6.** Ask the other person for permission to speak with them.

**7.** Say what you have to say, based on the facts, and with warmth and respect.

To confront someone, as I am defining it, is nothing more than bringing the information that you feel is important to another person for their consideration. You can't control their response, but if you make the communication warm and personal, as well as honest and factual, you increase the potential for a mutually satisfying experience, and possibly a solution.

## ⏱ TIME TO TAKE ACTION

1. Prepare yourself mentally. Take some time and review the facts. Try to reduce the emotional energy you are putting into this. Chapters 2 and 3 can help you with this. Use factual information that accurately describes your concerns. If you think your emotions are too strong, talk the matter over with someone you trust.

2. Be private about your confrontation. Don't confront someone in a hostile environment or in a place where others will hear you. Be considerate enough about their feelings, and you might see them return the favor. Be humble.

3. Start your information exchange by saying, "Do you have a moment to talk?" Before you delve into your presentation, obtain the other person's willingness to engage in the discussion. If they don't have the time right away, try to schedule it for another time.

4. Communicate in precise statements. You want the other person to clearly understand what you're saying.

5. Try not to worry about the other person's response. They may or may not agree with you. Your only concern is to become more efficient at presenting your concerns to others. Results are never guaranteed.

6. Stay away from trying to "get back" at that person in your mind. You do this by reducing your emotions as much as you can. Refer back to the list in Chapter 4 if you need help with this. You can also ask someone close for help if revenge is something you are considering.

7. Be willing to take a risk. You want to become someone who is capable of intelligently confronting problematic situations. Be that someone.

##  DRIVING IT HOME

We become more confident by learning to engage in healthy confrontations with other people. By keeping our emotions at a minimum, staying close to the facts, and using a warm, respectful approach, you will see that you are able to express your concerns, and that you won't lose your sanity in the process.

**YOUR DECLARATION IS**: *I will think it, I will plan it, I will say it.*

##  ONWARD

Conflict doesn't have to be a byproduct of anger. It is nothing to be feared, and it is essential to human growth. In the next chapter, I'm going to present some practical ways to incorporate the intellectual gift of conflict resolution into your life.

# CHAPTER 17

# Understanding the Value of Warm Conflict Resolution

## SAYING GOODBYE TO THE WAR ROOM

*Conflict is not the monster you make it out to be. It is an intellectual gift. It helps you organize your world, and tells you how intelligent you can be. You need to stop fearing it.*

---

**PROCESSES TO EMPLOY:** Present/Understand/Fix, Brutal Honesty, I Over E, Slowing Down Life's Pace, Conflict Resolution, Listening, Risk-Taking, Fact-Finding, Humility, Warm Confrontation, Positive Language Reciprocity, Communication

---

THE PROCESS OF CONFLICT RESOLUTION IS A powerful instrument in human growth. The standard definition of "conflict" is a serious disagreement or argument, typically a protracted one. That, unfortunately, is exactly how conflict is viewed. The view of conflict is packed with negative energy, and quickly conjures up horrible apparitions of emotional demons yearning to feast on our souls.

Conflict is neither positively nor negatively charged. It simply means that each party has different information. We, fearing the potential for loss, put the emotional charge into the information, certain that tragedy is going to bestow itself upon us. Thus, it's not the conflict that causes the problem, it's the emotional magnum opus we created that breaks our spirit.

# Win at All Costs

In classic conflict situations, there is an agenda to win the argument, and the intellectual weaponry being used is not always straightforward and honest. Engaging in conflict can make us feel as though we are stepping into the lion's den to have part of our humanity viciously ripped away. This is hardly the case. So, I'll redefine conflict using terminology that isn't delivered at the end of a blood-wielding sword.

*Conflict is the intellectual state that occurs when two different opinions occupy corresponding cognitive space at the same time.* The information is initially introduced as fragmented, oppositional, and incongruent. In conflict, the solution or compromise has not yet been defined. That may become the conclusion when the conflict is resolved. Conflict, then, as I am using it, simply means that two or more people are expressing information that is not the same.

Let's take a closer look at what happens when two people enter into a conflict. Since each person's opinion has been expressed, and both know what the other thinks, they are simply two people who have different opinions about something. Each person is aware that the information exchange could develop into an emotionally charged argument. So, even before any information exchange can occur, each party is poised for the potential of war. This happens because we all believe that the conflict will have a winner and a loser. This view of conflict is archaic. Consider this example:

## THIS IS WAR

Jake is a staunch Democrat. His whole family is, and always has been. He is in a heated discussion with Frank over a hotly contested social issue. Jake is towing the Democratic line, while Frank is holding down that of his Republican party mates. Each continues to deliver opinion after opinion, and the argument continues to become more heated. Finally, Jake leaves the argument, delivering one last jab, and exits the room. War was waged without compromise or solution, and in the end, neither understood what the other had to say.

This is an example of the conflict war room, complete with all its weaponry. If they were more willing to listen to what the other had to say, ask some questions, and give each other the respect due, things might have turned out much differently.

## Bad Rep

Before you can resolve conflicts between two opposing information sources, you must reduce the internal conflict you, yourself are experiencing. You need to stop fearing conflict, and become comfortable with the thought of opposing information sharing space with yours. That can be a good thing. Now I'm getting to the crux of our current discourse. Conflict is not always negative. Conflict can also be a positive intellectual experience, and that is the first conflict you need to address. That the human mind could even comprehend the existence of conflicting information reaffirms the magnificence of our cognitive capabilities.

Conflict is simply your mind recognizing that not all the information is complimentary, and that the way you present it needs to be revised. The human mind possesses the ability to accomplish the task, and it wants to do this. So, then why is there so much fear and insecurity when it comes to conflict resolution? The answer is our old nemesis: our emotions.

## Nothing But a Simple Intellectual Exercise

As I discussed in Chapter 3, the human brain is equipped with readily available tools to help you address both the internal and environmental issues you experience on any given day, and in any given situation. Conflict is essential to human growth. Expressing yourself efficiently in conflict situations should be nothing more than *unemotional presentations of simple facts*. An opposing viewpoint does not make one an enemy.

The real enemy comes from right inside yourself. Since your mind and emotions work so closely together, the line between intellect and emotion can quickly become blurred. In the heat of the battle, emotionally expressed opinions can become worthy of waging war over. When emotional barrages subdue the sound presentation of the facts, the result can be a dramatic, passionate battleground that soon bears little resemblance to the initial information. For this reason, emotional conflicts are rarely, if ever, resolved. Hence, you have a proven existential basis for your fear of engaging in conflict-related situations.

To further refine our definition of conflict, I am going to apply it to healthy conflict resolution. *Healthy conflicts are solution oriented, intellectually expressed exercises, that define and organize relevant information into cohesive, functional presentations.* As you can see, there is little, if any, room in this formula for the emotional weaponry of the war room. Let's look at our previous example, this time, with the concept of healthy conflict resolution in play.

Jake, the Democrat, and Frank, the Republican are engaged in a discussion over a hotly contested social issue. Each toes their own party's company line, but each is willing to listen to what the other has to say. Jake started the discussion with his version of the facts. Frank listened intently, and presented his own views. Jake reciprocated, listening to Frank, and the two men continued to talk and listen as the conversation developed.

In the end, there were some subtle changes on each man's part, and both men understood the other person's point just a little bit better. There wasn't a winner or loser, no one became angry, and each man respected the views of the other, though they didn't necessarily agree with each other on all of them.

Conflicts do not produce anxiety. Emotions do. Emotions have no place in conflict resolution, and you must set your sights on solutions, not worthless, petty skirmishes. In any opposing information design, there is the information, the willingness to discuss that information, and the resolution. Everything else is emotional rubbish. You speak, you listen, you respect, you attempt to compromise, and you move on. It's a simple information exchange, and you are all capable of using this wonderful intellectual gift.

##  TIME TO TAKE ACTION

1. When you engage in any conflict situation, make the decision to be honest, humble, willing to review the information, and dedicated to a solution. This sets the foundation for the communication necessary to resolve the conflict.

2. Keep your emotions at a minimum. Infusing emotion into an intellectual discourse does nothing but cause problems. Flip back to Chapter 4 for help with this step.

3. Focus more on the information being presented, and less on how you feel about it. It's the information you need to resolve the conflict. Keep those facts moving in the direction of a solution.

4. In a conflict, there is a tendency to go off track just a bit. When this happens, refocus on the facts, as you learned in the discussion on fact-finding (see Chapter 2). Keep your intentions focused on a solution.

5. Rid yourself of any preconceived notions about what might happen. Tell yourself that you're going to stay in the moment (see Chapter 8). This will help you stay close to the communicative process and the facts.

6. Keep the pace of conflict resolution slow and the volume low. Speak to the other person as a friend.

7. Try not to be so impassioned about how you believe the conflict needs to be resolved. Always remain calm, and always stay on topic. Never make the conflict evolve into a personal assault. If you can't remain calm, leave the situation—warmly.

8. Remember, you have no control over what the other person says or does. Focus on what you are saying, and be willing to listen to them. That's all you can control.

 ## DRIVING IT HOME

Recognize conflict as the powerful, positive tool it is. Feelings are important, and if possible, can be included in an intellectual discourse, but never, under any circumstances, do they rule the exercise. Through the Process Way of Life, you are learning to be solution oriented. Stay focused on that goal, and get out of the war room.

**YOUR DECLARATION IS**: *I will speak; I will listen; I will understand; I will compromise.*

 ## ONWARD

Anger is one of the most efficient ways to bring unhappiness into your life. In the next chapter, I'm going to present the faces of anger, and show you how you can reduce anger's impact on your life.

# CHAPTER 18

# Anger Games

## LEARNING AN ANGER-FREE WAY OF LIVING

*Since you only live once, it is essential that you live right. Live without anger, so you can appreciate your world.*

---

**PROCESSES TO EMPLOY:** Brutal Honesty, I Over E, Present/ Understand/Fix, Slowing Down Life's Pace, Eliminating Toxic People, Settling Past Issues, Communication, Listening

---

WHEN WE THINK ABOUT ANGER, WE TYPICALLY visualize someone who is verbally abusive or doing something physically aggressive. These are certainly expressions of anger, but they don't tell the whole story. There are many faces of anger, and to understand its far-reaching potential, I'm going to explain how we use this devious tool to protect ourselves, and to control others.

Anger comes from many sources, the most prevalent being past pain, frustration with other people, stress, disappointment, abuse, rejection, and abandonment. Sometimes, you become angry simply because you aren't getting what you want. In this chapter, I am focusing on how anger can affect you, interferes with the internal balance you are seeking, and what you can do to remove, or at least lessen its effects on you, and those you love.

# The Faces of Anger

Let's take a look at some of the different types of anger. The list is not exhaustive, but it does present the more common ways we use anger in our lives:

- **AGGRESSIVE ANGER**—verbally or physically abusing another individual.

- **HURTFULNESS**—violence, including sexual abuse and rape, child abuse, verbal abuse, biased or vulgar jokes, using foul language, ignoring people's feelings, willfully discriminating, blaming, and labeling others.

- **BULLYING**—threatening people directly, persecuting, insulting, pushing or shoving, using power to oppress, shouting, playing on people's weaknesses, and social-media attacks.

- **THREATS**—frightening people, finger pointing, fist shaking, and wearing clothes or symbols associated with violent behavior.

- **VENGEANCE**—punishment or revenge exacted for a perceived injury or wrongdoing.

- **OVER-PUNISHING**—giving an unrelenting punishment to an individual that is not in realistic proportion to the magnitude of the offense.

- **DESTRUCTIVENESS**—destroying objects, vandalism, hurting animals, reckless driving, substance abuse.

- **UNJUST BLAMING**—accusing other people for one's own mistakes, blaming people for one's own feelings, making accusations.

- **PASSIVE-AGGRESSIVE ANGER**—behavior that seems to be void of anger, but one's actions are designed to inflict pain on another individual, like the silent treatment, or hiding someone's personal property.

## Any Anger Will Do the trick

As you can see, there are many types of anger, and many of us display some of them from time to time. It really doesn't matter which type of anger you employ in your life. All of them can cause damage to you and the targets of your anger. You use anger for many reasons, such as:

➤ For revenge

➤ To manipulate and control others

➤ To reduce fear, or to hide it, and to mask insecurities

➤ To get our own way

➤ To avoid feelings of victimization

➤ To abuse others

➤ To feel more powerful

➤ Because you cannot control it or stop using it.

Anger makes you feel more powerful, or at least keeps you from feeling as though you might be taken advantage of or victimized. You may be conscious of a person or event that hurt you, or you may have repressed that pain to the point that you no longer understand it. In addition, you may attach your anger to people and situations in your life who are not associated with the instigating person or event. It may be difficult for you to understand your anger, because there is so much emotion associated with it. Also, other emotions are involved, such as, fear, disgust, sadness, and contempt, which can mask anger.

## Taking No Prisoners

Anger does not discriminate. Anyone can fall victim to angry outbursts and angry ways of living. Anger can go from 0 to 60 in a matter of seconds, or it can simmer, and then rise to a boil without notice. It can be passive, yet sophisticated enough to do its dastardly work, and remain invisible. It embarrasses, inflicts pain, destroys relationships, involves itself with the legal system, and the more drastic examples, kills others, or even its host.

Those who use anger often say that doing so allows them to vent, and often feel empowered. Some will talk about it as a motivator, and something that provides them with more self-insight. Others say they have more clarity of thought when they are angry, but this probably has more to do with the adrenaline rush it produces, though it is short-lived. Regardless of any of the temporary benefits associated with anger, its destructive value far outweighs any short-term quasi-positives.

## The Telltale Signs

You can recognize if you are angry, or if you are using anger, by the imbalance it causes in your four internal attributes. Take a look:

➤ Intellectually, expect more conflict and confusion. Irrational thought is also a byproduct of anger, as is obsessive thinking, and difficulty organizing and implementing plans.

➤ Emotionally, you have less control, and you can be difficult to reason with. You blame other people, lie, become obstinate, and are over-reactive.

➤ Physically, you may experience an elevated heartbeat, breathing issues, including hyperventilation, angry outbursts, destructive behavior, abuse directed toward others, and a general inability to remain calm. Your body seems to be going too fast.

➤ Spiritually, you will feel a drastic disconnection to the tranquility and peacefulness that your spiritual attribute provides.

➤ Anger can become a controlling factor in your life, but it doesn't have to define you. There are ways to address it.

## The 7 Ways to Fight Anger

1. Resolve your past pain.

2. Identify the anger you are using.

3. Define the source of your anger.

4. Never use anger as a tool to manipulate or hurt someone.

5. Define any fears which your anger may be hiding.

6. Be brutally honest with yourself, and don't blame others for your anger.

7. Get help either from someone you trust, or a counselor.

In the Process Way of Life, we look for longevity and sustained growth, shun quick fixes, and want to remain internally balanced. Anger is the "fox in the process hen house," devouring the health and internal balance the Process Way of Life teaches, and it can be quite difficult to stop, once you become proficient using it. Address it before it devours you.

## More Than a Habit

One of the most important dynamics of any addictive process is that once something becomes an addiction, we lose sight of why we started using it in the first place. Addiction is a neurological condition. You can perform the addictive behavior simply because you are addicted to it, and it alters the way you feel. Anger, just like drugs, alters brain chemistry, and gives you that rush that you may seek in your life. As a result, you may begin to use anger in situations where anger should never apply.

Once brain chemistry changes, you may introduce situations that can cause you to become angry, simply to feel the rush. When you do, you will feel pain relief, believe that you have more confidence, feel as though you have reduced your anxiety, and mistakenly believe that you are more efficient in your daily life. All of this comes from the neurological rush that anger provides, that altered brain chemistry we often see with substance abuse. Make no mistake about it, anger can behave just like a drug, and the loss of control can be astounding.

When anger gets to this point, and has become addictive, attempting to stop using it, like any other drug, will induce a period of withdrawal. This can cause depression, anxiety, and more anger. To determine if you have addictive anger, ask yourself the following questions:

1. Do I feel more confident when I'm angry?

2. Do I like the rush I get when I'm angry?

3. Am I getting angry in situations where anger is not necessary, or should not apply?

4. Do I routinely use anger to make me feel better in some way?

5. Is it difficult for me to stop being angry on my own?

If you answered yes to most of these questions, anger has probably changed the way your brain is functioning. It's a good idea to see a counselor. A counselor will help you understand why you're using anger, about the addictive process, and can help you formulate a plan to address your anger. This will help you avoid withdrawal symptoms, and assist you in establishing a plan to move forward without this destructive tool.

## ⏱ TIME TO TAKE ACTION

1. Anger can cause us to move swiftly. Slow your life's pace (see Chapter 5), and take a step back. Catch your breath and look at your options. There is always a healthier way to address the situation than to behave aggressively.

2. Be brutally honest with yourself. An important step in addressing your anger is to admit that you are angry. Everyone has some form of anger. There is no point in hiding yours.

3. All anger has a source. Don't deny or ignore that source. Identify it, so you may address it. If this is difficult, get help. Speak to a counselor, if necessary.

4. Know what kind(s) of anger you are using, and why. Refer to the list in this chapter. Identifying and understanding your anger can help you reduce it.

5. Stop blaming your anger on others or other situations. Difficult people and situations will always be there. Learning how to understand and address your anger begins when you are willing to look at yourself, not just others.

6. If you really feel that the source of your anger is a toxic person, you can address the situation with them, distance yourself from them, or terminate the relationship. A counselor can help with this if you need more assistance. I'm discussing toxic people in detail in Chapter 19.

7. Get the facts about the situation. Anger is an emotional rollercoaster. Keep in mind that we never solve anything with our emotions. It's always intellect over emotion that works best (see Chapter 4).

8. Don't buy in to the notion that anger makes you more powerful. In the end, it will always be your undoing. Power comes from healthy intellectual functioning. Find yours there.

9. Anger can become addictive. If you feel yours is, professional help is strongly advised.

 ## DRIVING IT HOME

If you think you are angry in some way, you're not alone. You do, however, have a choice. You can remain angry and experience everything that goes along with it, or you can do something about it. No one has the power to make you angry. You have a choice regarding the way you respond in any situation. Addressing anger is a huge step in creating a life that is happy, loving, and fulfilled.

**YOUR DECLARATION IS**: *I will live without anger, so I can embrace my world.*

 ## ONWARD

Who and what enters your life can have a profound effect on what happens to you. Only you control who and what enters your life. I'm going to look at gatekeeping next.

◇◇◇◇◇◇◇◇◇◇◇◇◇◇◇

# CHAPTER 19

# Deciding Who Gets In, and Who Stays Out

## The Cosmic Gatekeeper

*You are the guardian of your body, your mind, your heart, and your soul. Only you have the power to decide who and what may enter your world.*

---

**PROCESSES TO EMPLOY:** Brutal Honesty, I Over E, Present/ Understand/Fix, Slowing Down Life's Pace, Boundary-Setting, Eliminating Toxic People, Gatekeeping, Housekeeping, Intelligent Decision-Making, Internal Focus

---

THE PEOPLE YOU LET INTO YOUR WORLD can have a dramatic effect on your life, and those close to you. A good friend is like an oasis in the desert, always providing relief and support. On the other hand, a toxic person can hurt you with their negativity, often causing pain and disappointment.

You were born the perfect version of yourself, and your decision to remain that way, in part, rests on your choice to become your own cosmic, loving gatekeeper. You must be the guardian of your own personal world. You must understand that it is you who decides who and what gets into your world, and who and what stays out.

## Dastardly Threats

The world we live in is full of toxic people. They can enter your life, often wreaking havoc there. Elementary science lessons demonstrate that even a drop of toxin can drastically alter the purity of an ecosystem. Your physical, intellectual, emotional, and spiritual attributes represent your personal ecosystem. Even the smallest threats can upset your internal balance. It is so important that you tenaciously guard who and what enters your complex, interconnected personal network.

## Red Flags and the Process Stop Signs

Very often, you will have an idea when some person or event should not enter your world. You will know this, because your internal attributes will respond. You may experience some physical unrest, intellectually we may feel a bit conflicted, emotionally, here comes the anxiety, and spiritually, you seem a bit disconnected. Any of these can be a red flag that some person or event should be kept at a distance. Red flags exist for a reason. Not everyone will do well in your personal ecosystem.

The Process Way of Life is designed around balance, and toxic people can seriously upset that balance. So, while you're guarding your personal universe, scrutinize potential entrants carefully. If you feel unrest on any level, back up a bit, and rethink your decision to let them in. This doesn't mean the person cannot gain admission into your world; it simply means that you need to slow down and assess the situation before you make that happen. The following table highlights some of the major definers for both positive and negative people. Though not an exhaustive list, it will provide a defining guide regarding who to let in, and who to keep out.

# NEGATIVE VERSUS POSITIVE PEOPLE

| Negative People | Positive People |
|---|---|
| Negative people are manipulative. | Positive people are friendly people. |
| They are critical and judgmental. | They are motivated. |
| They're defensive and undependable. | They are complementary. |
| They can be closed-minded. | They tend to be open-minded. |
| They are demanding, wanting their way. | They enjoy connecting with other people. |
| They often have a difficult time when you're enjoying yourself. | They look for the positive in everything and everyone. |
| They don't forgive easily. | They like to be in service of others. |
| They are masters of one-upmanship. | They are honest. |
| They have more, and know more. | They are goal oriented. |
| They resist new perspectives. | They are grateful people. |
| They often go into victim mode. | They are people who like to learn. |
| They gossip and spread lies. | They take time for others. |
| They never seem to fully accept you. | There happy for others good fortunes. |
| They resist new approaches. | They put others first. |
| They are not caring or supportive. | They are usually easily approachable. |

## Protecting the Journey

As you proceed in the Process Way of Life, you're going to be making plans that will bring you to your goals, and enhance the quality of your life journey. It's so important that you don't allow the owners of the red flags to penetrate the healthy and productive journey you are creating. Just as one ounce of toxin can poison an entire ecosystem, one unhealthy person or event that you allow to become part of your life can have the same effect.

You're using the Process Way of Life to enhance the quality of your life. You are ridding yourself of what does not belong in your life, improving what you already have, and you have life goals. You simply cannot allow anyone to interfere with the quality, productivity, and enjoyment of your life journey.

For toxic people who are already in your life, especially in your home, like parents, spouses, siblings, and children, the decision is a little more difficult, but not impossible. Though you can remove toxic people from your life when they do not live with you, those who do present a different set of circumstances. It might make sense to talk with someone to help you with this. A close friend might help, or you may want to think about a professional counselor to help you make some decisions.

Remember, these processes are helping you learn to trust yourself, which depends so much on becoming and staying internally balanced, and reducing the effect of toxic and dysfunctional external forces on your internal attributes. If you are going to be successful in developing and maintaining your happiness, your powers of thought, and your ability to maximize your potential, you need to understand that in your personal cosmic universe, you must become a tenacious gatekeeper.

Being a master of your own destiny, you choose who and what may be part of your world. With open arms, you extend loving invitations to those who are a positive influence in your life, and you quickly remove those who are not. It's just one more important way to love yourself, and protect the person you are becoming.

 ## Time To Take Action

1. Make conscious decisions regarding the people you want to include in your life. Refer to the list above as a guide.

2. Make every attempt to include positive people and situations in your world. Positive inclusions usually yield positive results.

3. Gatekeeping helps us establish the boundaries you need to keep your life positive and productive. Guard your boundaries closely. I'll be exploring boundaries in Chapter 21.

4. Establish standards for yourself, and make sure others meet these standards before you grant them admission into your world. The list above can get you started. Make your own list; write it down. Then, by all means, live by it.

 **Driving It Home**

It's up to you to decide who will be part of your life based upon your own love for the person you are, and your willingness to accept the responsibility to protect yourself. You were born the perfect version of yourself. Become your own cosmic, loving gate-keeper, so you can stay perfect.

**YOUR DECLARATION IS:** *It's my journey; in with the positive, out with the negative.*

 **Onward**

Protecting your life journey and all the growth you are realizing is important, but sometimes it can be difficult to let those who love you in. Making some adjustments in your personal walls by learning to trust those you love can be life-changing, as you'll see next.

◇◇◇◇◇◇◇◇◇◇◇◇◇◇

# CHAPTER 20

# Walls, Isolation, and Trust

*The walls you build to protect you keep others out, but they also keep you isolated and alone on the inside. Take a risk. See what's on the outside!*

---

**PROCESSES TO EMPLOY:** Brutal Honesty, I Over E, Present/ Understand/Fix, Slowing Down Life's Pace, Communication, Internal Focus, Risk-Taking, Trust

---

OUR BRAINS ARE SPECIALIZED MASTERS OF DEFENSE. They routinely employ sophisticated strategies that keep us from getting hurt as threatening situations arrive in our lives. The success of those strategies depends on the brain's ability to perceive those events as they are occurring.

So, how would this sophisticated neurological system address the possibility that a threat may find its way in and hurt us? By now, you've probably heard the adage, "The best defense is a strong offense." Our brains employ a system that is always on guard, but remains undetected.

## Invisible, but Influential

The defense system I am talking about operates "under the radar." It's like your computer's operating system, one that employs a virus detection program. When activated, the program services the computer, but you never see any signs of it. You can navigate between one program and another, and if the virus protection program is running properly, it protects your computer, but you never realize it's there. It only notifies you if a threat is detected. Let's explore what such a format would need to do:

1. It will need to protect you from threats you do not realize are occurring.

2. It would have to subtly let others know that there are boundaries, and that you prefer those boundaries not be violated. (Boundaries will be discussed in Chapter 21.)

3. It would have to allow you the flexibility to socialize, form relationships, and reach your objectives without compromising personal information you wish to keep private.

4. You should also be able to increase and decrease the strength of this format consciously.

5. There is one system that accomplishes all these needs. It is the walls you employ to keep people either at a distance, or from crossing the boundaries you've established for yourself. A wall, as I am defining it, is an automatic, protective internal structure that resides in both the conscious and preconscious centers of your brain. It is designed to protect you and your privacy. I'm calling this a *preconscious* process since you do not have to engage conscious thought to enable it. Yet, it can transition to a cognitive state, which means that you can control it, and subsequently make some decisions regarding how strong it is. Like your computer's virus program, it runs in the background, never seen, but you can open the program and adjust its settings to accommodate your needs.

## Hiding in Plain Sight

Let's take a closer look at how a wall operates in your daily life. I'll start with *conscious walls*. Conscious walls surround something you are deliberately protecting, something you're not letting anyone in deep enough to connect with. Examples might include an event from your past, a fear, or some part of yourself you want to keep secret. You might use such a wall to protect you from a security breach, that is, someone getting too close to the item you are protecting. The wall may be in operation consistently; however, you use minimal resources to maintain it until a threat is realized. This helps you conserve resources until they are needed. Remember energy distribution is important, so we don't want too much of it being distributed to a wall which may not be needed at the present time. You typically have a significant amount of control over your conscious walls, since you are aware of how, why, and when you are using them.

The second type of walls are preconscious. They lie just below the level of immediate conscious awareness, and serve two purposes.

➤ First, as with their conscious counterparts, they protect you from threats you are aware of.

➤ Second—and this is where it gets interesting—a threat does not have to be present, and in fact, you don't even have to feel the possibility of a threat for them to be operating.

A well-constructed preconscious wall helps you establish the appearance that all is well, and that you are at peace with your surroundings. It readily projects how you appear to, and are known by others, while protecting personal information hidden behind the wall. Most people will not identify, let alone, understand the disguise. However, those who are more intimately connected to you might ask questions as they begin to detect that you may be hiding something. This is where interpersonal problems can arise. Here's an illustration.

Tom and Jen are in the initial phase of a new relationship. Tom's father was a warm and loving man, but emotionally protective. He rarely let his guard down for anyone, including his wife. Tom's mother understood this, and rarely challenged the boundaries his father established. Tom is self-employed, having a landscaping business, and spends a large amount of time alone.

Jen is one of three children, coming from a more open family background. She communicates well, and openly discloses the more intimate parts of her life. She works as a counselor in a state-run rehabilitation center. Tom and Jen have been seeing each other for four months, and the emotional part of their relationship is becoming more intimate.

Recently, Jen has begun to feel that there's only so close she can get before Tom becomes evasive. He changes the subject, injects humor into the dialogue, and has even responded by saying he doesn't know what she was asking. As far as Jen is concerned, her questions are simple, straightforward, and don't require a tremendous amount of introspection. As Jen pursues the situation, Tom begins to show more reluctance, and he seems to be getting annoyed.

Many of us have either experienced Jen's frustration, or we may be like Tom, and are reluctant to open ourselves to a potential threat. Tom may say that he doesn't understand what Jen is asking for, and he may be telling the truth. The reason for this is simple. Since Tom's walls are preconscious, he is not controlling them consciously, and they have become his normal way of behaving. He may not realize that the walls are there. He may even tell her this. He too, is becoming frustrated. Tom may be wondering why she keeps pressing on with her concerns about his evasiveness. "After all, aren't things good the way they are?"

By the time your walls have become a routine part of your life, the reason for their existence is well hidden. They become your personal norm. In fact, when presented with the possibility that they exist by someone close to you, you may respond by saying that you don't know what they're talking about. A wall is a security device designed to keep intruders out. It doesn't necessarily understand that someone who loves you is not an intruder. The quality of your relationships may suffer, since the wall keeps your loved ones at a distance.

So, how do you know if a) you are using preconscious walls, and b) if they may be causing problems for you? You likely have preconscious emotional walls if you can say the following:

1. For reasons unknown to me, I am protective when it comes to sharing personal information, even when it's not that threatening.

2. I employ other devices like humor and misdirection to keep others from getting too close.

3. I may avoid situations where any type of serious conversation about me may begin.

4. I may become uncomfortable and even abrupt if I am pushed to disclose information that I'd rather not disclose.

## Prisoners in Disguise

Using walls can protect you from personal harm, but becoming a prisoner behind them is an entirely different story. A wall should possess the ability to serve you, but never control you. You should never become a prisoner, stuck behind your walls, and have difficulty understanding yourself. Also, a wall shouldn't keep healthy people from connecting with you.

If you think you are using some of these strategies to protect yourself from others who may be getting a little too close emotionally, it's a good idea to begin with a conscious approach. Ask yourself if there's anything that has occurred in your past that may cause enough stress for you to keep it under wraps. Sometimes, going back and talking to people involved in past situations can help.

If you're uncomfortable with intimate communication, use tactics like diversion, avoidance, humor, or anger to keep significant others at bay, it could be signaling a problem. If you were raised in a home where self-disclosure was difficult, discouraged, or not permitted, attempting to let someone in can activate the wall without an understanding of why this is happening. You might have simply learned to use walls. Now, you like being "personal." Being this way seems normal, but it can make you a very lonely person behind your personal defense system.

Your goal is to be healthy, and have your attributes operating in a state of balance. For this to happen, you want to gain control over your preconscious walls, so they don't interfere with the development of the healthy person you are creating. Take a risk. Come out from behind your personal security system, and introduce yourself to the rest of your world. It doesn't bite, and it's loaded with new options and new choices. This one comes under the heading of expanding your horizons.

 **TIME TO TAKE ACTION**

1. Identify and put closure on past issues. This reduces the need for the walls, and helps you come to terms with parts of yourself that can cause pain, and subsequently, isolation. Again, talk to the people involved, and get help if necessary.

2. Walls, by their very nature, hide honest information. Fact-finding is essential here. Be brutally honest. See Chapters 2 and 3.

3. Though walls tend to be expressed through our intellects, they are emotional creations. The process is I Over E. You want our intellects to examine information first. See Chapters 4 and 5. Slow down, and let your brain catch up with your feelings. Entertain the possibility that you are, in fact, using walls, and try to understand why you are doing so.

4. Defenses are always involved in the construction of a wall, especially denial. See which ones you may be using. Flip back to my list of defenses in Chapter 14.

5. Understand that there is a difference between a wall and a boundary. Healthy boundaries help promote internal control, as you will see in Chapter 21. Preconscious walls can rob us of that control. Know the hows, whens, and whys associated with your walls.

6. Take a risk, and let someone you trust closer than you usually do. Then, assess how you feel when you do. If you begin to become uncomfortable, it's a good idea to try to understand why. A wall only treats the symptom. It never efficiently addresses the problem. Get help from others you trust, or a counselor if you need it.

 **DRIVING IT HOME**

No one needs to be open about themselves with everyone, but openness, honesty, and a willingness to share one's life with loved ones creates the peace and the connectivity human beings desire and need. A huge and wonderful world is waiting for you on the other side of your wall.

**YOUR DECLARATION IS:** *My walls come down; my happiness goes up.*

 **ONWARD**

Setting personal boundaries is necessary for your overall health. But just as important as setting healthy boundaries is learning how to defend those boundaries. The next chapter will assist you with these essential processes.

◇◇◇◇◇◇◇◇◇◇◇◇◇◇◇◇

# CHAPTER 21

# Setting and Defending Your Boundaries

*They love to rearrange your life. They are the boundary thieves.*
*Remove your lines from the sand, and take your life back.*

**PROCESSES TO EMPLOY:** Brutal Honesty, I Over E, Present/
Understand/Fix, Slowing Down Life's Pace, Boundary-Setting,
Conflict Resolution, Eliminating Toxic People, Gatekeeping,
Intelligent Decision-Making, Truth-Telling

OUR THOUGHTS AND BEHAVIORS BELONG TO US, and other people
should not have the right to willfully cross our personal boundaries
without our permission. Boundaries are different than walls because
we consciously set them not only to protect ourselves, but to help
us to define how we want to live our lives. We are always aware of
them, and they are a valuable asset to our personal health.

We all have boundaries, but some of us are better at defending
them than others. The goal of this chapter is to help you understand
how to establish healthy boundaries, how to communicate them to
others, how to defend them when necessary, and how to change
them for the right reasons.

Personal boundaries openly communicate how far we are willing to extend ourselves with any person, and in any given situation. Boundaries are personally set limitations. We establish them
for others to see and respect. We incorporate boundaries into our
lives primarily for physical, intellectual, and emotional control, and

sometimes, to keep us safe. Boundaries may also reflect our personal preferences.

## Setting the Limits—Boundaries In Balance

Most of us have a reasonable idea regarding how close we want others to get to us. The magnitude of the boundary typically differs depending on how much trust we have in the other person. Most of the time, we can communicate our boundaries to the significant others in our lives, and they will respect our boundaries. But that's not always the case. The "boundary thieves" like to violate our boundaries by pushing past them, usually against our wishes, or without our understanding.

Setting healthy boundaries supports our four balanced life attributes.

➤ Physical boundaries are often interpreted as not being touched when you do not want to be touched, and in a way that you do not want to be touched. A physical boundary can also mean a defined amount of space that you prefer others not violate.

➤ There are intellectual boundaries in which information about yourself is something you prefer that others not know.

➤ There are emotional boundaries where you are protecting your feelings, and you're not as willing to share those with others, since they may leave you open and vulnerable.

➤ Spiritual boundaries may include not allowing verbal spiritual attacks, such as being told you are unintelligent because you believe in something you can't prove exists, or because your spiritual belief differs from the mainstream.

To set efficient boundaries, you're going to use your four internal attributes.

➤ Physically, you incorporate boundaries into your life to protect your body. No one should have the right to touch you unless you are giving them permission. Additionally, never allow anyone to restrain you, strike you, or be physically violent with you in any fashion. You must also make decisions about those who may touch you and how they may touch, even if your boundary thieves are well-meaning.

> Intellectually, you will have boundaries which surround what information you keep inside, and what information you allow to become public. This is a simple conscious evaluative process where you decide how much you want to disclose about yourself or anything about you.

> Emotionally, you have feelings, and those feelings need to be respected. It's important to establish how much of your emotions you are going to make available to others.

> Lastly, your spirituality protects the core of your inner peace. Let no one willfully attack your spiritual preferences.

Let's look at some of the things you can do to set healthy boundaries.

## The 7 Principles of Healthy Boundary Setting

1. Examine the facts relevant to any person or situation.

2. Keep your emotions to a minimum, and your decisions based on the facts.

3. Go slow, so you may examine information productively.

4. Look for those red flags, and exercise caution in potentially toxic situations.

5. Be brutally honest in your assessment of others. Make no excuses for them.

6. Make a personal likes-versus-dislikes list. Use it to start setting your boundaries.

**7.** Once you set your boundaries, stick with them. Let no one violate your boundaries, or coerce you into changing them.

It's important to understand what you think and how you feel about the people in your life. You've already formulated feelings about others from the facts you previously gathered about them. From this information, you establish how far you are willing to go with others, and how close you are going to let them become with you. Stay close to the facts you have gathered to set healthy boundaries.

Boundaries can be all-encompassing, such as those related to morality and honesty, or they can be very specific and may reflect thoughts or feelings about specific subjects or people. Simply ask yourself how you think, and what you feel in those situations, and begin applying your boundaries there. If you feel any anxiety or unrest, you need to slow down, reevaluate the information, and decide how you're going to move ahead. Talking it over with someone you trust can help.

## The Secretary of Defense, and Healthy Boundary Expansion

It would be foolhardy to think that just because you set boundaries, others are going to respect them. The rest of the world isn't always making a commitment to grow along with you. They may not be so willing to respect your personal borders. As you are setting boundaries, you must be willing to take on the role of defender of those boundaries.

Setting a boundary is only the first step in the process. It's important to you, and it's a healthy decision to make, but other people can't be counted on to be part of your plan. This may occur inadvertently, or they may very consciously choose to violate your boundary. At the very least, they may try to help you to expand it to accommodate their desires. You don't establish a boundary only to have someone else tear it down. When this happens, it's a clear indication to them that their assault can work, and they will try it again.

Peer pressures, relationship issues, personal insecurities, fears, risks, and a variety of other motivators can cause you to expand or eliminate a boundary under pressure. Never buckle to the pressure. You, and you alone set your boundaries, and you, and you alone make the decision to change them. You can change a boundary because you don't need your former plan anymore, but always have an intelligent plan to do so. That's healthy boundary expansion.

## Expanding the Territory

The only time a boundary should change is if *you* decide to change it. If you're going to change a boundary, give it some thought first, and have a plan to do so. For example, say you never wanted to get a tattoo. You felt that it was unsanitary, made you look cheap, or that it might not be received well by family members. Now you're considering the possibility of getting one. It makes good sense to research the issue to determine the pros and cons of the process. Then, you might decide where you want to go to get one, how big it should be, and where on your body you'd like to have it drawn. Here, you are expanding a boundary, but you are doing so backed by an intelligent plan. This is what I call healthy boundary expansion.

The choice to expand the boundary is not the problem. Doing so under pressure, and doing so without a plan is an entirely different story. If you're going to expand a personally set boundary, do so only because you want to. Don't let someone talk you into it, and never allow someone to pressure you into making a choice that runs counter to a limit you have previously set. Peer pressure is the most efficient boundary killer. It causes conflict and insecurity You, alone, make a boundary changing decision, since you alone have to live with the choice you make.

## Telltale Signs

As always, if your boundary is being expanded, either by you, or by someone else, and it's not a healthy choice, or if you're doing so without a viable plan to make it happen, you may feel some unrest.

- Physically, you may experience yourself going a bit too fast as your body reacts to an accelerated pace.

- Intellectually you will feel some conflict since the information may tell you that something is not the way it should be.

- Emotionally, you might feel some anxiety as your emotions begin to take over.

- Spiritually, your inner peace is reduced.

Think your boundary expansion process through, make sure that the reason you are making the change is healthy, and have a plan to move forward. Use your intellect, be honest with yourself, go slow, and get the facts. Move forward only when you feel comfortable about your decision. This is expanding your boundaries the right way.

As you grow, expanding boundaries is a natural progression. Boundaries are normally set at certain times in our lives because that's what we needed at that time. As we grow, however, we change the magnitude and the scope of those boundaries to coincide more realistically with our capabilities. So, a decision to change a boundary should reflect growth, better understanding of self, and increases in personal security and self-esteem.

## In Defense of Yourself

Any good boundary needs a good plan of defense to enforce it. Here's a simple example: You have a candy jar on your desk in your office. Each morning, a few fellow employees, without permission, raid your stash. Unhappy with this behavior, you tell everyone that you would prefer if they would ask your permission before they indulged themselves. The next day, more candy is missing, and no one has asked your permission. This now requires that you reiterate your position to them in no uncertain terms, including what may happen if they repeat the behavior.

You'll need to enforce what you have verbalized. That doesn't mean you have to become angry or scream at people. You just need to, once again, verbalize your initial assertion, and let the other people know you are unwilling to move from that point. Then, don't move. If others feel that you are an easy mark, and that you can be swayed to abandon your boundary, they will continue to make attempts to help you reset your boundaries to meet their needs. They, however, usually give up once they see that you aren't the pushover they thought you were. These are your boundaries, not theirs. Keep it that way.

Boundary establishment and defense take time. You need time to think, to plan, and finally, to defend your boundaries. Setting boundaries is a conscious intellectual exercise. It requires intelligent thought, and as I've presented throughout the Process Way of Life, it requires time. Never go fast with your boundaries. In fact, that's how the boundary thieves tear them down. They try to make you go too fast, which reduces your time to think about what you're going to do.

Always verbalize your boundaries, as you saw in the example. Let others close to you know where you stand, and how far you're willing to go regarding a specific matter. Try selecting a few people in your life whom you trust, and begin the process with them. Tell them what you think, how you feel, and how far you're willing to go in any situation. This will help you to start setting your boundaries with safe people, and in safe places. You can branch out to others from there. Boundaries don't have to be etched in stone for you, but they are for others. It's your life. You make the decisions; not them.

 **TIME TO TAKE ACTION**

1. Examine the information that's important to you. Set your boundaries based on that information, and then verbalize your boundaries, in no uncertain terms, to others. Keep in mind that the strength of your verbalization will communicate how important that boundary is to you. You're not asking their permission not to cross your boundary. You are telling them that it cannot occur.

2. No one has the right to violate your boundary, but do expect that this will happen. Be ready to defend what you are verbalizing. Simply reiterate your point, let the boundary thieves know that there will be no movement, and that you are happy right where you are. Using the example of the office candy jar, should the boundary thieves continue to take the candy, tell them that if they do, the jar will be removed, and if they repeat the behavior, do so.

3. From time to time, you may choose to expand your boundaries. Make that a part of your personal growth, and a conscious decision after a review of the necessary information. Have a plan to do so, one that protects you, and one that also allows you to enjoy the new territory that will become part of your life, just as I discussed in the case of getting a tattoo. Always refer it back to your processes. You'll find the ones you need listed at the beginning of each chapter.

4. Keep the 7 Principles of Healthy Boundary Setting in mind. Use them to establish and defend your boundaries.

5. Understand that if you are expanding a boundary which may work against you, you will feel the negative charges coming from your physical, intellectual, emotional, and spiritual attributes. If this happens, slow down, and review the facts. Rarely, does anything good happen fast.

6. If you are going to allow a boundary thief to violate your boundary, be ready to accept the consequences that come with relinquishing control of that part of your life *to someone who is being insensitive enough to take it from you.*

7. Don't feel guilty about refuting a boundary thief. Usually, they get over it, but you have no control over that. You are setting your boundary for a reason. It's important to you. That's what you need to be concerned about.

## DRIVING IT HOME

Boundaries serve the important purpose of teaching others to respect you, and they help you to respect yourself. Good boundary-setting and defense of those boundaries have the added luxury of helping you to realize that you are important, and that if you are willing to treat yourself as such, others will treat you that way as well.

**YOUR DECLARATION IS**: *I will live in my space, according to my rules.*

## ONWARD

Now that you are working hard to set healthy boundaries, you'll want to make sure you don't fall into the trap of people-pleasing. As I will present next, there's no need to overextend yourself simply to give others what they want.

◇◇◇◇◇◇◇◇◇◇◇◇◇

# CHAPTER 22

# People-Pleasing and Emotional Survival

*Remove others from the center of your life. Be the center of your world, and your own perfect life force. Work outward from there.*

---

**PROCESSES TO EMPLOY:** Brutal Honesty, I Over E, Present/ Understand/Fix, Slowing Down Life's Pace, Boundary-Setting, Conflict Resolution, Dignity, Honor, Internal Focus

---

THROUGHOUT THIS BOOK, I HAVE BEEN STRESSING how dangerous it is for you to allow yourself to be influenced and controlled by other people. In this chapter, I'm going to look at the misaligned behavior of people-pleasing. When you people-please, you find yourself doing your best to make other people happy, while at the same time avoiding anger and conflict at all costs. A people-pleaser is *a person who wants everyone they are associated with to be happy and content, and they have decided that they will be responsible for the way others think and feel.*

## Peacemakers

There are two concerns I have for people-pleasers. The first is that it's so difficult for them to be themselves at any given time. Doing so might "rock the boat," causing others to become angry and displeased, either with them or some other person or situation. People-pleasers are typically nonconfrontational toward others, so their way of addressing the situation is to "make it go away." Instead of calling another person out for what they're doing wrong, a good people-pleaser attempts to alter the situation by altering their own behavior. The long-range prognosis for this type of strategy is quite poor, since it does not address the cause of the problem.

My second concern for people-pleasers is that they are rarely, if ever, honest with others, or themselves. They seldom address the real cause of the problem. They have decided that if they appease the other person, that person will react differently, and difficult situations will be avoided. They are also trying to control people, events, and situations in which they, themselves, are uncomfortable or insecure. People-pleasers want everyone to like them, all the time.

People-pleasing is an extremely subordinate way to live life. People-pleasers spend significant amounts of time assessing other people's needs and moods, and sacrifice who they are, and what they believe, to make sure that other people are satisfied. It doesn't take long for others to realize that people-pleasers place their dignity and self-respect in other people's hands. When this occurs, we see the development of behaviors in these people that are no different than so many other bullying and abuse situations.

People begin to take advantage of the people-pleaser, since they understand that their disparaging and often disrespectful behavior will not be confronted. In the end, people-pleasing becomes a survival condition onto itself. When it's all said and done, the people-pleaser is no longer altering their behavior to please another person. That person has little respect for someone who so willingly surrenders their dignity. People-pleasers are now pleasing for their own emotional, and sometimes physical survival.

## Maid to Order

Codependency is another very important factor when it comes to people-pleasing. I'm defining codependency as *an excessive emotional or psychological reliance on another person*. Many of us have a very difficult time thinking for ourselves. Codependents need the approval of others, and put another person at the center of their lives. As long as that person is happy and displays positive gestures and feelings toward them, their world remains centered and balanced on its axis. Should that person be "having a bad day," then their world spins erratically out of control.

Codependents are masters at assessing other people's behaviors. It's the fundamental concept that makes pleasing other people functional. Unfortunately, while people-pleasers become so proficient at assessing and defining other people's needs and behaviors, they lose sight of their own, forget who they are, and are rarely, if ever, capable of addressing their own needs. Consequently, they become dependent on the happiness being displayed by the object of their people-pleasing. Consider this example:

## IN SEARCH OF DIGNITY AND SELF-RESPECT

Miah and Judd have been married for twenty years. Miah is a very accommodating person who loves to please other people, and is always willing to go that extra yard to make them happy. Judd, on the other hand, is a self-centered individual, who puts himself first, and rarely overextends himself to address anyone else's needs. Judd can be verbally abusive, and often criticizes Miah. Having lost her self-respect, Miah remains consistent in her attempts to please her husband, but the more she tries, the worse he seems to get. He no longer respects her, realizes that he can verbally abuse her, and has no problem doing so in front of other people. In attempting to please Judd, Miah is losing her dignity, her self-respect, and in the end, nothing has improved between her and her husband.

Not unexpectedly, people-pleasing causes a severe loss of personal identity, self-honesty, individuality, and independence. When you depend so intensely on the feedback you are receiving from another individual, you willingly sacrifice your own needs. When all is said and done, it's your own dignity you're giving away. You are doing this simply to obtain the positive feedback you think you need from that other person.

It's difficult to see people-pleasing as a detrimental process while you are engaged in it, because you firmly believe that you are doing something positive for someone else. This makes you feel good about yourself, and camouflages the loss of identity and dignity, which will, as the situation progresses, cripple you. Also, we are taught from our formative years to be kind to others, and, in our personal relationships, to put the needs of the other person before our own. This makes it difficult for people-pleasers to see that what they are doing is damaging them.

The rule of thumb is: you do for others when they cannot do for themselves. You allow them the dignity of their own independence so that they, themselves, may master the art of their own personal growth. To this end, people-pleasers not only destroy themselves. Their enabling can have a serious negative impact on the people they believe they are helping.

How can you tell if you are a people-pleaser? Here are the important questions:

➤ Are you doing things to make other people feel good when you know it may not be the right thing to do?

➤ Are you overly concerned with what people will think about you if you make your feelings known?

➤ Are you doing things to avoid confrontation or disappointment from others?

➤ Do you make excuses for other people's behavior, knowing that they are wrong?

➤ Are you willing to do the wrong thing to make someone else feel right?

➤ Are you afraid to express your own opinions to other people?

➤ Do you need others to feel good so you can be at ease in your life?

➤ Have you put dysfunctional people in a position to control your life?

If you answered yes to these questions, you may want to consider what effect people-pleasing is having in your life. If you stop the people-pleasing behavior, you will experience some discomfort because your insecurities will increase, but that's temporary.

Also, others may want you to continue to perform for them. If there is no threat of violence or any other abusive response, it's a behavior you can stop. If there are violent or abusive overtones, you definitely need some help. Don't be afraid to get it. Counselors are quite adept at bringing you through this. At the very least, it's time to stop cowering to others. Stop allowing yourself to be someone else's overaccommodating subordinate. You're better than that.

##  TIME TO TAKE ACTION

1. Realize that your life is important, and that you have choices. Everything else depends on this.

2. Understand that you will never, ever please everyone all the time. Make sure that whatever you choose to do is something you feel comfortable doing, and that it's the correct action to take.

3. Your choice to help resolve a difficult, angry, conflicted, or dysfunctional situation is always admirable, but never compromise the person you are to make that happen.

4. Remember, you decide who comes into your life. If you must change yourself to please someone else, do you really want them to be part of your journey?

5. In any situation, you need to know how far you are willing to go, and you alone set those limits and boundaries. Never allow anyone to set or cross them (see Chapter 21).

6. Be sympathetic and empathetic, but always be assertive and let people know where you stand. Focus on the problem, and never take responsibility to be everyone's fixer.

7. Never apologize for something that another person does. You can't lose a friend you never had, and if you must sacrifice who you are to please someone else, they weren't your friend to begin with.

8. If you think you need to leave a relationship that has you in a subordinate position, and you are cowering to please someone, get help. See a counselor if you're not sure what to do. It's a first step that can change the rest of your life. Without your dignity, what good are relationships? Do love them, but love yourself, too.

 ## Driving It Home

People-pleasing is often a symptom of self-esteem and victimization issues. If you're struggling with your decision to stop people-pleasing, don't be afraid to ask for help. No one should ever have to be in a subordinate position to another person, and no one should have to cower to another human being. You are beautiful, and you are important. Never forget that.

**YOUR DECLARATION IS:** *My dignity comes first; the line forms there.*

 ## Onward

The way you use language is so important, both to you, and in your communication with others. It directs your thoughts, expresses what you think and feel, and it communicates your thoughts, needs, and feelings to others. I'm going to show you how to use language to help you create the person you want to be, and to better communicate that to others next.

# CHAPTER 23

# Language Reciprocity and Fulfilling Communication

*Words can control your thoughts, and change the thoughts of others. The way you speak to yourself and others sets the stage for how you live your life.*

---

**PROCESSES TO EMPLOY:** Brutal Honesty, I Over E, Present/ Understand/Fix, Slowing Down Life's Pace, Communication, Fact-Finding, Listening, Living in the Moment, Positive Language Reciprocity

---

LANGUAGE ACQUISITION IS THE PROCESS BY WHICH humans acquire the capacity to perceive and comprehend language, as well as to produce and use words and sentences to communicate. This chapter turns your attention to the intellectual and emotional effect language has on you, and your interpersonal relationships.

We use language to state and clarify our position and opinions, to connect with others, and to gain information in a wide variety of formats. We can instill fear with our words, or we can express love. We can speak from our hearts, or we can lie through our teeth. We can draw people in, or we can push them way out. We can use language to educate, or we can use it to confuse. We can speak with straightforwardness, or we can be conniving and manipulative. Language is one of the more powerful tools you will use on your process-life journey.

# The Inner Voice

Humans think with language. You use language to communicate with yourself, just as you do with others. Language is not only the byproduct of what you think, it also helps to create, define, and redefine the way you think. An angry person is more likely to have negative thoughts. If your internal language is negative about yourself, the people in your life, or your environment, you may come to believe what you are thinking, and may adopt that as your own identity.

If, however, you make a conscious effort to talk to yourself using positive language, your words have the capacity to help you create positive feelings about yourself. The way you think and the way you feel are so intimately interwoven. Likewise, the way you think and feel usually equals the way you behave. So, the language you use, primarily with yourself, will eventually translate into who you are, and how you represent yourself to the rest of the world.

## Master and Slave

Language doesn't only describe what the brain thinks and feels, it often tells the brain what to think and feel. Language can tell your brain to feel good about something or someone, or it can define your world using aggressive and negative terminology. Sometimes those thoughts are consciously applied, but over time, the way you speak to yourself can become your own linguistic autopilot. The following table illustrates the difference between positive and negative internal language.

## INTERNAL LANGUAGE

| POSITIVE INTERNAL LANGUAGE | NEGATIVE INTERNAL LANGUAGE |
|---|---|
| Things are good in my life. | I hate my life. |
| I can do that with a little effort. | Nothing I do ever turns out right. |
| I think people feel good about me. | No one likes me. |

| I have what I need to succeed. | I never get what I need. |
|---|---|
| People are inherently good. | People are inherently evil. |
| I feel good about myself. | I don't like myself. |
| If you give people a chance, they will come through. | If you give people an opportunity, they will hurt you. |

Typically, you spend a significantly greater amount of time in your own mind than you do in the external world. If you are spending a large amount of your internal time with negative language, it creates a negative version of yourself, and it influences you to live that way. When, however, you learn to use language to be a positive thinker, it becomes an ally for you. You are what you think, so you need to be thinking healthy thoughts.

We are social beings, and communication is paramount to our survival, and the quality of our lives. For the purposes of the Process Way of Life, I am defining communication with others in two ways:

1. The imparting or exchange of information.

2. A means of connection between people.

We can use language to manipulate our environment, but we can also use language to connect to other people in ways that foster nurturance and trust.

## Subtle Force or Warm Connection: Using Linguistic Nuances

Language is one of the primary vehicles to show your respect for others, as well as to communicate with them. I've discussed how important being respectful to others is. With this in mind, I am purposefully moving past exploring the need to respect others. I am instead going to concentrate on some of the simpler linguistic nuances that you can use to enhance the quality of your communication with other people.

I'm describing linguistic nuances as *subtle shades of meaning or expression in our communication with others.* They are the little things you can say, the delivery you use, and the softer, less noticeable communicative gestures you can employ to enhance your communicative experiences. Since you can use language to both influence your thoughts, and to connect with other people, it's important that you learn a kinder, more thoughtful linguistic approach.

The following table contains both positive and negative linguistic nuances. They will help you understand how the little things you do can affect the way you communicate.

## USING LINGUISTIC NUANCES

| Positive Nuances | Negative Nuances |
| --- | --- |
| Relaxed body language | Anxious body language |
| Good eye contact | Poor eye contact |
| Smooth, easy flow | Communication interrupts |
| Clear concise statements | Ambiguous statements |
| Low volume | High volume |
| Listening to others | Evidence of not listening |
| Reinforcing statements | Critical statements |
| No agenda evident | Hidden agenda evident |
| Accepting statements | Demanding statements |
| Warm language | Aggressive language |
| Respectful language | Condescending language |
| Open to others' opinions | Closed to others' opinions |
| Soothing voice | Agitating voice |
| Relaxed disposition | Anxious disposition |
| Open to discussion | Can be argumentative |

## Positively Speaking

Positive communication is an honest, straightforward, and truthful presentation. It doesn't have agendas, and allows the other person the dignity of expressing their own opinions in an environment where each party feels understood and respected. Here are a few suggestions that might be helpful in your future dialogues.

## The 7 Pointers for Positive Communication

1. Present your information accurately. Be direct. Don't try to lead anyone to your conclusion.

2. Give others a big-picture presentation that is factual. Try not to become more emotional if you don't seem to be getting through to them.

3. Focus on the present—that is, your communication process, and enjoy that time.

4. Don't have any hidden agendas, and respect what others have to say as they are responding. Their opinion is important, too.

5. Don't focus on the goal and the happiness or disappointment you may be feeling once you get there. Focus on facts, the process, and on warmth and respect.

6. Listen to what your communication partner is saying. Listening is essential in good communication. You need facts, and listening is how you get them. Listen intently, and always be responsive to what others are expressing.

7. Try to stay away from "reloading" while they are talking. Don't focus on what you plan to say next. Listen, and respond with a genuine interest in what they are saying.

Language does indeed have a powerful influence over the way you think, how you behave, and how you communicate. Regardless of whether you are using language internally as you think, or in your interactions with other people, being positive and kind begins internally, and finds its way outside to your environment, and those whom you share that environment with. Speak with positive language internally, and express that kind of language with everyone you touch.

 **TIME TO TAKE ACTION**

1. Make a concerted effort to stop thinking in negative, aggressive, angry, and toxic terms. Use positive internal language.

2. Replace the toxic way of thinking with thoughts that are accurate and honest, and put you in a position to acquire the correct information about yourself, and any situation you may find yourself in.

3. Start retraining your brain to use positive language both by consciously focusing on positive self-verbalizations, and by correcting yourself when negative thoughts are expressed. Positive affirmations like "I like what I'm doing" or "That makes me feel good" are examples of positive ways to talk to yourself.

4. Practice positive vocalizations with friends and family. Enter any conversation with the notion of keeping your mind positive and your expressions representative of positive feelings. Be mindful of those small linguistic nuances. Though small, they can have a powerful impact on the way you communicate.

5. Avoid negative verbalizations at all costs. It's hard to take your negativity back once you make it public.

6. Set aside enough time so that your communication is not rushed. Efficient and respectful communication never moves swiftly. Keep the pitch of your voice relaxed, and don't rush what you are saying.

7. Make the communication process more important than your agenda. You want to enjoy communicating with others.

8. Listen intently to what your communication partner is saying. Stay away from reloading, and always be responsive to what others are expressing.

 ## DRIVING IT HOME

Learning to use language to influence positive thoughts in yourself and others can open the door to a way of life that creates and continues to maintain healthy thought processes and positive relationships. It's also one more way to be kind to yourself. Communicate warmly to yourself, and to others. Speak to yourself as though you love yourself. Speak to others the same way.

**YOUR DECLARATION IS**: *I will think positive, I will speak positive, I will stay positive.*

 ## ONWARD

As you put your life goals in perspective, it allows you to see what is important in your life, and what causes clutter in a needless acquisition process. In the upcoming chapter, I'm going to explore needing less to have more.

◇◇◇◇◇◇◇◇◇◇◇◇◇

# CHAPTER 24

# Keeping Life Simple

## NEEDING LESS TO HAVE MORE

*Riches have nothing to do with what you acquire. They have everything to do with the realization that you already have everything you need.*

**PROCESSES TO EMPLOY:** Brutal Honesty, I Over E, Present/ Understand/Fix, Slowing Down Life's Pace, Intelligent Decision-Making, Keeping Life Simple, Life on Life's Terms, Living in Today, Living in the Moment, Journey Living, One-Day-at-a-Time Living, Reduction of Destination Living

THE HUMAN FRATERNITY, ESPECIALLY IN SOCIETIES THAT have all that they need, and much of what they desire, has a tendency to confuse needs and desires. As you will see, there is quite a difference between these two value points in your life, and the way you approach them can drastically affect your health, your happiness, and your potential for growth.

### NEEDS VERSUS DESIRES—PART 1

List *everything* you think you need in your life on a blank piece of paper. Do this before reading ahead. Likely, your list includes items like:

➤ Food

➤ Water

- Shelter
- Clothing
- Health care
- Friends and family
- Education
- Employment/ adequate finances
- Hobbies
- Smartphone upgrades
- Transportation
- Entertainment
- Vacations
- Social media
- New car with the bells and whistles
- Going out to eat

Hold on to this list. You will be revisiting it later.

## Round and Round We Go

The purpose of this chapter is to help you examine what you need in your life versus your desires, those items you feel are so important, but you don't necessarily need. I also want to help you understand that acquiring unnecessary desires may not necessarily increase your happiness. In fact, it may become the chains that bind you to a toxic and neurotic style of living, which is so often the antithesis of the happiness you thought it would produce. I call this style of living the "acquisition merry-go-round." This is *the continuous and obsessive cycle of emotional investment for unnecessary personal gain.* It possesses no productive purpose, and produces no long-term, sustainable happiness and fulfillment.

The old saying that simple pleasures are the best couldn't be more on target. That's because these types of pleasures are uncomplicated. When you overemphasize the need for grandiose acquisitions or on repeatedly having to acquire something that is not essential, you can become a slave to the acquisition process. The acquisition process must be repeated so that it may reinforce the notion that you are going to satisfy your desire for something you have defined as a need, but which is simply not essential. It's window-shopping your way through life with a fantasy payoff.

If you convince yourself that a nonessential desire is a need, you can justify overindulging and overspending to engage in the activity. Regardless of whether or not you successfully acquire what you want, you will have wasted important time, energy, and resources to acquire something you simply did not need, and you have conned yourself in the process.

## Bells, Whistles, and the Joneses

Effort is defined as *the process or resources it takes to acquire something*. The amount of effort should be in direct proportion to what you are acquiring. Effort includes, but is not limited to, time, finances, family, labor, and responsibilities. You don't want to spend more time acquiring something than you should. If something is worth acquiring, doing so shouldn't affect the quality of your life in other areas. So, by our definition, you should only be expending effort that coincides with what you're acquiring, and what you are capable of acquiring. You just don't need the stress that goes hand-in-hand with keeping up with those Joneses, and a continuation of life on the acquisition merry-go-round, which is slave inducing, and never-ending; all for items you don't need, and this is our central theme.

## Invisible Chains

Let's explore what can happen to you when you become a slave to the process of acquisition. "Slave" is the watchword here. The question is how much are you willing to surrender, and how much internal freedom are you willing to sacrifice to acquire what is not necessary? The effort, that is, the price being paid, all too often far outdistances the joy received from ownership. This amounts to selling your soul to the "acquisition devil." The concern is that it can become such a natural process, but since it comes with "rewards," you don't recognize it as slavery.

Slavery doesn't have to include cracking whips and steel chains. In fact, the most difficult chains to break are the ones that can't be seen. It doesn't feel like slavery, because the perceived pot of gold at the end of this foolish carnival ride catches you in its invisible snare. It creates the illusion that this self-surrendering process was worth the mirage that you viewed as its treasure. Nothing in this world is worth the selling of your soul. More important, nothing is worth reducing yourself to slavery.

The interesting point about this meaningless fiasco is the blind willingness people can display to become part of a never-ending cycle of meaningless acquisition. They beat themselves up, feel worthless, lose important resources, destroy relationships, live in a perpetual state of envy and debt, and every day, until they get that little pot of gold, they are miserable. There is a very steep price to pay for wanting what you don't need, especially when you're willing to sacrifice your own peace of mind and happiness for acquisitions that may be insignificant, and in the long run, worthless.

## NEEDS VERSUS DESIRES—PART 2

Now, take your list out, and divide it into two columns: needs and wants. It should look something like this:

| NEEDS | WANTS |
|---|---|
| Food and water | Social media |
| Shelter and clothing | Smartphone upgrades |
| Family and friends | Vacations |
| Education/vocational training | Entertainment |
| Employment/adequate finances | Hobbies |
| Transportation | New car with the bells and whistles |
| Health care | Going out to eat |

As you can see, the items under **Needs** are essential to your routine daily life. It's important to have them, and some of them are related directly to your physical survival. Others will add safety, and the ability for you to move forward and be more productive. The items listed under the **Wants** section are those that you typically think you need, but really if you had to, you could do without. The point of the table is to clarify needs versus wants, and to help you understand that the majority of your resources should be used to attain what you need in life.

Assess how much effort you are using to secure items on your need list. In today's economy, it's a significant amount, but they are needs, and you can't do without them. Now, take a close look at your want list. These are the things you want, but don't necessarily need. Wants should never be classified with such severity. Compare how much effort you are expending on that second list. Be honest with yourself, and take a good look at:

➤ How much the process of acquisition is costing you for these unneeded, but so dearly cherished items.

➤ How much better life could be if you didn't over-expend your resources and your energy attempting to acquire items that you don't need.

➤ How much happier you'd be without the chains that are binding you to the acquisition process. Think about how unhappy you can become until you acquire these foolish amenities.

➤ How much more on your need list could be acquired with the energy and resources you are expending to acquire the items that you do not need.

Do you have that rainy-day money? How much of any debt you have is a result of the desire/acquisition process? Is your retirement being efficiently addressed? The list goes on. Never focus your attention on the continuation of an acquisition process that establishes yet one more foolish, but empty destination in your life. Focus your energies on what you need. There's nothing wrong with directing some of your energy toward items you desire in your life.

The concern is that you don't make these priorities. Look at them for what they are. They are nothing more than quick fixes. In the Process Way of Life, we turn a cold shoulder to quick fixes, always remaining focused on growth and happiness for the long run. With that in mind, needs always trump quick fixes, and satisfying short-term desires coming from life on the acquisition merry-go-round.

Try to keep your desires at a minimum. Don't keep yourself in the pitiful position of chasing unnecessary desires as a way of life. It will do nothing more than cripple your life's journey. Focus on what you need, and keep your life simple. Love yourself enough to avoid this never-ending, slave-based wasteland. Live a simpler life, and get off the acquisition merry-go-round.

 ## TIME TO TAKE ACTION

1. Take the lists you created in this chapter seriously. Take a good, hard look at the difference between what you need and what you want.

2. Take an honest look at how much time and resources you are spending on your want list. Purge yourself of what is unnecessary and causes you to fall short with respect to securing the items on your need list.

3. The acquisition merry-go-round is nothing more than destination living. Keep it about your day-to-day journey. Chapter 7 explains this.

4. Understand that the process of worthless acquisition is indeed a form of self-abuse and slavery. Never put yourself in a position to pay for something you don't need.

5. Everything you own requires energy to maintain it. Decide how you want to expend your energy, and where you need to expend it. Discard what is using energy that you can apply elsewhere more efficiently, and with less anxiety.

6. Understand that to be rich means to be without meaningless desires. Focus your energies on becoming rich on the inside.

7. Never rationalize your needless acquisition process. Stay within your means, and don't lie to yourself. Don't tell yourself, for example, that you absolutely need social media. That's not a need. It's a desire. Don't lie to yourself on this one.

 ## Driving It Home

Imagine being able to say, "I have everything I need, and that's good enough." Visualize the peace you will experience when you are no longer a slave to your own unnecessary desires. Live simply. Let every day be one where you are happy with what you have.

**YOUR DECLARATION IS:** *I will acquire less on the outside, so I can be rich on the inside!*

 ## Onward

We live the journey moment to moment, but we can also include goals in the plan without them becoming time-stealing destinations. I'm going to discuss how to turn destinations into healthy goals that add a positive twist to your life journey next.

# CHAPTER 25

# Setting and Achieving Goals

## DESTINATIONS REDEFINED

*Look forward to all the wonders that life has to offer, but have a plan to make them happen, and make each and every day part of that plan. Make your journey come alive.*

---

**PROCESSES TO EMPLOY:** Brutal Honesty, I Over E, Present/ Understand/Fix, Slowing Down Life's Pace, Commitment, Fact-Finding, Goal-Setting, Incremental Forward Movement, One-Day-at-a-Time Living, Time/Energy Management

---

I DISCUSSED THE DIFFERENCE BETWEEN journey-oriented people and destination-oriented people in Chapter 7. While it's important to enjoy as many moments of our lives as possible, destinations can also be a positive and healthy part of our lives. In this chapter, you'll learn how to turn destinations into goals, with a practical way to achieve them. It's about evolving from a dreamer to a doer, and making this process part of your life journey.

## Destinations Redefined

Destinations can help you feel good about yourself, and help make your life journey that much more enjoyable. It's nice to include them in your life, but you don't want them to have an adverse effect on your life journey. To help you do this, I am going to redefine "destinations" as goals. Goals are *a person's aim or desired result, something you might like to have or achieve at some future time*. The trick is to establish an intimate and compatible marriage between your routine daily life, and the goals you may have: that is, to include them as a healthy part of your life journey.

Unlike destinations, which can simply be future arrival spots, goals are systematic plans that give you something to aim for, however, without sacrificing the wondrous excitement of the moments of your life as they unfold. Instead of merely focusing on some future destination, you are going to learn to establish a plan that helps you achieve future goals, while also allowing you to enjoy all the moments you are investing in your forward movement right up until your goal is realized.

It's a good idea for you to have **long-term goals**, like something you want to accomplish or places you want to be, maybe four or five years down the road. They don't have to be written in stone, but they do help you formulate a direction for what you want to accomplish in the future. An example of a long-term goal may be "In five years, I'd like to own my own business." This is a long-term goal. It's going to take some time to get there, so you'll need some **short-term goals** that will lead you to the long-term goal. Short-term goals have two functions:

1. They can assist you in your movement toward your long-term goals.

2. They can act as goals themselves.

Examples of short-term goals that may relate to setting up a business might be saving $5,000 or getting a business management degree. Both of these short-term goals can help you to establish our own business; however, both of them are goals themselves. Your short-term goals will require **action steps**. An example of an action step might be to schedule an appointment with the bank to establish a business account to start saving that $5,000. That step is always carried out in a defined time frame to help ensure that it is addressed.

# Your Goal Grid: Making the Dream Come Alive

To illustrate a format that includes long-term goals, short-term goals, and action steps, I am going to use a goal grid. A goal grid is easy to prepare, and allows you to see your entire goal structure. The grid is laid out with the long-term goal at the top. Under the long-term goal are three short-term goals to help you arrive at the long-term goal. Under each short-term goal are three action steps. These action steps are necessary to achieve the short-term goals. Action steps are always stated in time frames, since the entire grid depends on these being carried out appropriately, and in timely fashion. Here's how a typical goal grid looks:

## MY GOAL GRID

| |
|---|
| **LONG-TERM GOAL:** to own my own organic pastry shop |
| **SHORT-TERM GOAL #1:** to get my associate degree in business management<br><br>*Action step #1: to save $100 for my college admission fee (one month)*<br><br>*Action step #2: to apply for admission to the community college (six weeks)*<br><br>*Action step #3: to be accepted at the community college (three months)* |
| **SHORT-TERM GOAL #2:** to get my car ready for the daily ride to college<br><br>*Action step #1: to save $150 for auto parts (one month)*<br><br>*Action step #2: to repair my car (one week)*<br><br>*Action step #3: to get my car inspected (one week)* |
| **SHORT-TERM GOAL #3:** to identify the appropriate classes to enroll in during my first semester<br><br>*Action step #1: to call the admissions and financial aid offices at the college (one week)*<br><br>*Action step #2: to visit the college website online to examine course selections (one week)*<br><br>*Action step #3: visit the college (one month)* |

As you can see, the long-term goal is to open an organic pastry shop. There are three short-term goals that our businessperson will use to achieve the long-term goal. Under each of the short-term goals there are action steps that also include time frames. As the short-term goals are achieved, they move the pastry-maker in the direction of the long-term goal. Once a short-term goal is achieved, a new short-term goal can be established along with new action steps to keep the process going.

It's important to be realistic with your short-term goals and to set realistic time frames for your action steps. This helps you avoid becoming discouraged if something takes longer than expected, or if you encounter some obstacles along the way that require you to adjust your time frames.

It is very helpful to make your goal grid an active process. Revise your goal grid as you achieve the short-term goals. Add more short-term goals as necessary to keep moving toward your long-term goal. Having clear action steps with realistic time frames helps you avoid procrastination, and all those little excuses you might use to avoid doing something you are now holding yourself accountable for.

## From Wishers to Doers

What separates the dreamers from the achievers are goals that have executable parameters. Your dreams will only come true if you are willing to formulate a realistic plan to get there, and keep yourself committed to that plan. You need to move beyond the dreaming stage, and into the practical application stage.

A goal grid allows you to see your plan. It allows you to set time-frames and achieve small goals, creating a functional route for you to arrive to your long-term goal. Most importantly, having a sound and readily executable plan keeps you action oriented, and committed to a process of change. Here's the best part. *Since the goal grid has you taking care of business every day, it becomes part of your life journey.* It's staying on the journey, with destinations redefined as goals, and realistic plans to get there, still loving your journey, moment by moment, and one day at a time.

## ⏱ TIME TO TAKE ACTION

1. Set a long-term goal, one that is realistic, and is something you would like to achieve.

2. Create a goal grid *in writing*, or *use an app*. Include short-term goals and action steps with time frames for each of the short-term goals that will bring you to your long-term goal.

3. Address each action step within the time frame you established to reach your short-term goal. When that goal is realized, move on to the next short-term goal.

4. Review your goal grid regularly. Adjust your action steps or short-term goals only if necessary. Don't make a practice of adjusting your goal grid to accommodate laziness and distraction. Keep yourself focused, and address the grid the way you laid it out.

5. Don't make excuses to avoid the work. Make the work part of your daily routine.

6. Make your goals become part of your life journey, and enjoy every second of the time it takes for you to make them happen. Dream, plan, then do!

##  DRIVING IT HOME

Setting a goal, having a plan, and watching that plan come together can be a gratifying accomplishment. At the very least, the process of setting goals complete with action plans can change the way you approach your life, and this change can be invaluable. Turn your dreams into reality, and make your journey come alive, one moment at a time.

**YOUR DECLARATION IS:** *I will dream my dreams; I will make them happen.*

 **ONWARD**

Get ready to be introduced to the awesomeness that has been hiding inside you just waiting to shine. It's time to get in touch with your creative side, and begin thinking like the truly creative person you can be.

◇◇◇◇◇◇◇◇◇◇◇◇◇

# CHAPTER 26

# Defining and Living a Creative Life

*You are not mundane or ordinary. There is a creative fire inside you. You only need to connect to it. Then, you can unharness the power of your imagination.*

---

**PROCESSES TO EMPLOY:** Brutal Honesty, I Over E, Present/ Understand/Fix, Slowing Down Life's Pace, Belief, Commitment, Creativity, Journey Living, Incremental Forward Movement, Positive Language Reciprocity

---

THE MERRIAM-WEBSTER DICTIONARY DEFINES "CREATIVITY" as *the use of one's imagination or producing original ideas, especially in the production of artistic work.* For the purpose of this discussion, I am presenting two levels of creativity. We see the more primary level of creativity as the mind works through situations that require problem-solving abilities, especially in new situations, and the higher level of creativity, abstract creativity, that unveils the more abstract areas of our imagination.

## The Concrete and the Abstract

When you understand both levels of creativity (primary and abstract), you can learn the process associated with harnessing your own creative abilities. This will assist as you attempt to push past your perceived limits and onward to achievements you never thought you could understand, let alone master. Grasping the magnitude of your own personal creativity further helps you understand that you are special and extraordinary in your own unique way.

The first level of creativity is *primary creativity*. We use primary creativity in our daily experiences that call for routine problem-solving. The second level of creativity calls for the ability to define and engage our energies at a more advanced level. It motivates us to be our own personal creative visionaries. This is *abstract creativity*.

I use the term abstract because we don't readily possess a concrete way to understand how to access it. Most of us routinely use creativity on the primary level. It's on the abstract level where things begin to become a bit more complex. I'll examine primary creativity first. The following example illustrates what happens when we need to call upon our primary creative abilities to bring a solution to a new situation.

## CREATIVE IN THE CITY

Kenny resides with his parents who own a small farm in Indiana. He leads the youth group at his church, and he would like to move to a bigger city when his college days are over. Though Kenny likes new challenges, he has never traveled beyond the state border.

Kenny has been invited to visit a friend in Chicago for the first time. He is driving into the city, and this will be a new experience for him. As he enters the city, he attempts to program the new destination into his car's navigation system. The system, however, fails to recognize the destination. Kenny makes several attempts to address his dilemma. They all fail.

Kenny decides to try a different approach in which he must use his creative problem-solving abilities, that is, his primary creativity. Kenny stops the car, and knowing that his friend lives a block from St. Michael's Hospital, he programs the hospital into the car's navigation system. This will take Kenny close to his destination, and put him into a position to find his friend's apartment. So, Kenny had to do something that required novel thinking. He had to create. This is primary creativity, and we routinely use this problem-solving ability to address routine daily-living situations.

We don't usually think of routine daily problem-solving tasks as an expression of our creativity. That's because they are, in fact, routine. We tend to assume that creativity is reserved for people like artists, and those who perform extraordinary feats. Nothing could be further from the truth. Most human beings are capable of complex abstract thought. This being the case, most of us are capable of abstract creativity. We all have the capability to be creators in our own right. We simply need to define the path that will take us there. That's what those who we define as creative did.

For many of us, it's difficult to define our own personal creativity. There are two reasons for this:

1. **Self-doubt**—We tend to believe we are not creative unless we do something extraordinary. When we do not excel or do not receive feedback that tells us that there is something special about our abilities, we label ourselves as routine, not special, and as a result, not creative.

2. **Comparison**—We compare ourselves to others who have been labelled creative. As a result, we find viable, concrete substantiation to support the notion that we are unremarkable. When this happens, we consciously decide to be mundane and routine. Then, we conduct our lives in fulfillment of the pedestrian, self-assigned prophecy that says that we will never be special, and never be creative.

This is such a defeatist way to perceive ourselves. This manner of thinking does not apply itself to our potential. Rather, it defines us as limited people who have given up on this part of ourselves. This should never happen.

The more traditional view of abstract is something that exists in thought or as an idea, but has no physical or concrete existence. Therefore, it can be difficult to connect with this part of our intellect. We tend to think in concrete terms. Abstract, as it is traditionally referenced, has little, if anything to do with solid physical form. So that you may begin to embrace our own abstract creativity, I'm going to redefine what "abstract" creativity is.

*Abstract creativity is the ability to supersede your perception of your own creative limitations, so you can define your own personal storehouse of applied imagination.* By this, I mean that all of you have in you your own personal and hidden repository of creative energy that has remained untapped. That creative energy is open and available to you whenever you choose to call on it. You simply need to learn how to make that happen.

## Metaphysically Speaking

I now turn your attention to the process of summoning your abstract creative energies. This is a twofold process, one that you will need to adapt to, and one that takes time to learn how to use.

➤ First, you need to begin the process of ridding yourself of negative thinking. I'm talking about those thoughts that tell you that either you are not creative, or that any attempt you make will probably fall short of your goal. Creative energy should always be positive energy. As such, negative thinking serves to distance you from your own creativity. If you choose to think about yourself as someone who is not creative or who may never be creative, you will not be creative. Your fate has already been sealed. Negativity, in any form then, has no place here.

In Chapter 23, I stressed how important positive language can be in helping you to feel better about yourself. To begin the process of removing negative thinking from your creative energy, talk to yourself in positive terms. Your positive energy then, can be reinforced regularly.

➤ The second part of the process concerns connectivity to creativity. Now, you need to understand that you can access your abstract creative energy, but you need to think of yourself as possessing the ability to do so, and you must tell yourself that you can make this happen. This does not mean that you will quickly identify some future achievement that will define you as creative. It just gets the process going.

All of life is a process, and that formula holds as true here as it has for every other topic I'm discussing in this book. The goal here is to define and understand the *pathway to creativity*. So many of you are trying to define what you are good at without first defining the pathway; the process that will take you there. Creative people thought of themselves as being creative long before they realized how they were going to express their creativity.

It's important for you then, to define your pathway to abstract creativity. To get started, employ a little cognitive reversal energy. Begin to tell yourself that you are creative, and that you possess the ability to do creative things. Positive thinking yields positive results. Next, you're going to go back to those baby steps. Instead of defining a goal, and then trying to induce creativity where you have never applied it before, you're going to apply as much creativity as you can to every little thing you do in your life.

Your process is to practice becoming a creative person, and to be consistently creative in small matters, even simple chores like washing the dishes or making the bed. You could sing along with a song from your playlist, or set down a few dance steps to add a spark to these mundane chores. Do something novel. Put your own personal spin on it. Add a little "style" to what you're doing. Do nothing in your life routinely. You think about it with creativity, and you do it creatively. Creative thinkers are creative almost all the time. Start with baby steps. Here's an illustration.

# TRANSCENDING LIMITS

Damien is a high school senior who has always wanted to be seen as a creative person. He excels in photography and art. He plans to attend college to study art, and recently started working with oil paints. Damien expects much from himself, and tends to set goals that require him to stretch beyond his creative boundaries. He has always wanted to be a painter. Being drawn to landscapes, Damien has tirelessly tried to paint them. He tends to compare himself to other great landscape painters, but this endeavor has been challenging for him.

This time, Damien has applied a different approach. He has decided to go back to the beginning. He starts by purchasing a paint-by-numbers landscape scene. Painstakingly, he completed his first project. Next, he purchased another paint-by-number landscape scene, this time replacing the colors with his own selections. He is now moving beyond the concrete form of creativity, and introducing himself to the beginnings of his own abstract level of creativity. He is beginning to think about himself as creative.

Damien follows this step with painting lessons with an artist specializing in landscapes, and someone who he sees as a creative person. After spending six months taking weekly lessons, Damien has begun to create his own landscape productions. He is confident, and sees that he is expressing himself with a form of creativity he never experienced before. In the process, he is moving beyond the concrete level of paint-by-number pictures, and into the more abstract elements of his own mind, now expressed through his own creatively infused paintbrush.

Creativity isn't just applied to magnificence. Creativity is magnificent, always! If you think about yourself as being creative, and apply creative thought in all you do, your results will be more creative, and you'll be reinforcing your feeling that you are creative. Let's say you are taking dancing lessons. The dance instructor teaches you all the dance steps for the hip-hop dance you want to learn. You can stop your progression there, or you can fuel your new dance with steps of your own, turning a simple repetitive endeavor into an over-the-top personal masterpiece. Apply this thought, and subsequently this way of living to everything you do.

There is doing it, and there is creatively doing it. It doesn't matter if you're painting a picture, doing the laundry, washing the dishes, playing a sport, or taking a walk. Put your own creative stamp on anything you do. You are unique, perfect onto yourself, and a living miracle. That's where your creativity was born, and that's where you're going to nurture it.

Be innovative and creative in everything, and in every moment of your life. Put your own personal creative stamp on your entire journey, one moment at a time. This process won't take hold right away, but be patient. Be willing to give it the time it takes to develop, and you will begin to see positive results. As you begin, keep it conscious. Never stop thinking about being creative. Consistently applying your creativity in the little things in your life creates the pathway to abstract creativity, and it makes your life journey so much more fun to live. You are already creative. Live it in everything you do! You got this!

 **TIME TO TAKE ACTION**

1. Remove all negative thinking regarding your ability to be creative. Never think about yourself as mundane or ordinary. Refer back to the steps in Chapter 23 to help you keep your thoughts, and subsequently, your creative energy positive.

2. Never compare yourself to people you consider to be creative. Their creative statement belongs to them. Your own creativity will be defined through the process of your continuous personal creative thinking.

3. As you think of yourself as a creative being, apply as much creativity to everything you do, every day. Something as simple as creating a daily to-do list can be a creative act. You can just scribble the items down, or you can "fancy-up" those letters. It's that easy to exercise your creativity. Be positive, and don't be afraid to be a bit silly. Have fun with this. Don't hold back. Abstract creativity is on its way!

4. Put your own personal creative stamp on everything you do. Creative people stamp everything they do with their own personal creative mark. Make a mundane impersonal chore yours by infusing it with a signature mark of your own. The dance class I gave you is an example.

5. Be patient, and stay committed. Damien defined his path. He went slow, and he took painting lessons. It will take you time, but it won't be long before you start to define your own personal creative pathway. Have fun with this life-changing process.

 **DRIVING IT HOME**

Redefining yourself as a creative person stokes the fires of your imagination, transforming you into a person who routinely challenges your limits. You can create visions that propel you beyond the ceilings that previously defined who you were. *Creativity is not a destination.* It's a process that becomes one more defining mark of your life journey. Rethink yourself into creativity and carve your new life out of your old wilderness. You are creative. Live that life!

**YOUR DECLARATION IS:** *I will think creatively; I will be creative.*

## ⚐ ONWARD

From creativity and into passion. Passion isn't just something you experience. It's something you create. It starts inside you, and moves outward to every part of your life. I'm going to show you what real passion is, where it comes from, and how it can change your life in the next chapter.

# CHAPTER 27

# Passion from the Inside Out

*Passion is an engaged state that permeates your entire being.*
*It never turns off, and it is felt even in the most subdued times.*

**PROCESSES TO EMPLOY:** Brutal Honesty, I Over E, Present/
Understand/Fix, Slowing Down Life's Pace, Internal Focus,
Keeping Life Simple, Living in the Moment, Humor, One-Day-
at-a-Time Living, Passion

WE USUALLY THINK OF A PASSIONATE PERSON as someone who is intense, emotional, excited, animated, and spirited—maybe even hot-blooded and energetic. Despite the emotional potency inherent in these attributes, and where they all possess some degree of passion, they have little to do with the definition of a truly passionate person.

We like to attach ourselves to situations that excite us. These may include a love interest or a vacation, a winning lottery ticket, or some hobby we enjoy. Then, there are those special life conditions, those that quickly raise our emotions, and get everything flowing inside of us, like seeing our favorite singer in concert, or watching our team win the big game. We feel captivated and are passionate about our lives, at least during that moment.

That you can become impassioned and apply that passion in your life tells you that you are alive and engaged in your journey. So, passion that comes from external sources can add some very nice experiences to your life. If, however, you define your ability to be passionate only through external, situational, and excitable events, it does raise some concerns.

When you become passionate about some exciting event, the way you are feeling passion is being expressed through external stimulation. It's an external shot in the arm that creates a heightened level of enthusiasm which adds a temporary passionate experience to your life. Now, if you only become passionate by experiencing some external stimulation, then we're really talking about a form of *situational passion*, that is, excitement.

*Internal passion,* on the other hand, *is a constant internal state that never turns off, penetrates every level of your existence, and applies itself to everything you think, feel, and do.* This brings us to the central point of this discussion: the difference between externally induced passion and passion that is constant and always alive inside you. The following table shows the differences between internally and externally passionate people.

## INTERNAL VERSUS EXTERNAL PASSION

| INTERNAL PASSION | EXTERNAL PASSION |
| --- | --- |
| Passion starts from inside | Passion starts from outside |
| External events not necessary | External events necessary |
| Passionate about everything | Passionate is situational |
| Never turns off | Is intermittent |
| Is about the journey | Is attached to destinations |
| Can attach to small events | Events more intense |

## Fire in the Belly

External passion is a response to some external stimuli that moves inward, having its primary impact on your intellect and your emotions; elevating both. For example, your baseball team is playing in the World Series. You are typically enthusiastic about the sport, but now your passions are enhanced, and your energy level has gone through the roof. You feel your adrenaline rushing through your body. You can't get enough of the whole affair. This is an example of situational passion.

We all experience these moments, regardless of whether we are externally or internally passionate, though an internally passionate person does not *require* them. Therein lies the difference. An internally passionate person can enjoy the excitement, but doesn't necessarily need the external stimulation. This is because their passion is born and nurtured inside of them. They love their lives, and they seem to be passionate about everything.

So, using our example of the big game, an internally passionate person will certainly become excited during the course of the game. They, however, don't need the experience, because they were already passionate about their life journey.

This is another example of having everything you need inside of you to live and be happy. Internal passion lives inside you, and is always active regardless of what you are experiencing. It routinely moves out to your external world. As such, it adds passion and excitement to everyone and everything you touch. Internal passion is all about loving the gift that is your life; all of it.

## The Slow and Constant Simmer

So, how do you become passionate about who you are? The answer is to become passionate about the process of growth—your own growth. Through the Process Way of Life, you've been learning to be more efficient intellectually, more stable emotionally, healthier physically, and more connected spiritually. This is where passion lives: in the processes you use to grow.

If you are dedicated to the process of internal growth, your movement forward will impact everything you touch and experience, and ignite a renewed sense of enthusiasm in you. The process of internal growth nourishes the senses, and allows for the healthy expression of your intellect, and your emotions. You feel better, and your life has enhanced clarity. All of this is a process, and this is exactly what you need to become passionate about: *your own internal process of growth, your Process Way of Life.*

Remember that adage about the people who are "high on life"? To be high on life, you need to be "high" about the internal part of your life, and love every aspect of your life, moment-by-moment. Nothing external can compare with internal passion. Thus, you don't require the external exciters. You can appreciate them, but you don't need them. You will already have passion; an all-encompassing passion that external events cannot match.

Now you can see why external passion takes a backseat to that which emanates from the inside. It simply does not possess the power to override the more global internal feeling created by *growth-driven internal passion*. Internal passion is who we are, always, while external passion is what we experience, temporarily. It's journey-over-destination living defined by internally driven passion that wraps itself around your entire existence.

Internal passion emanates from inside you, and works its way outward. It is a dynamic part of your Process Way of Life journey. Love every minute of the new person you are becoming. Be passionate about your new growth, and use your own internal passion to define and give life to all that touches you. Laugh and have fun. Make your life a passionate process-based life journey. Live every moment of your life with passion in its truest form. Touch the world and everyone in it with the passionate person you are becoming.

##  TIME TO TAKE ACTION

1. Passion is inside you, and this potential has always been there. Choose to embrace this wonderful internal process. Appreciate, and be passionate about your whole life.

2. Focus on the processes that are helping you grow. Be passionate about your growth, and those processes that are helping you to realize that growth. Flip back to the list of processes in the beginning of the book regularly to help you apply them.

3. Be excited about externally passionate situations, but enjoy them as just another part of your passionate life journey.

4. Attach enthusiasm to everything you do. Be passionate about your life, and everything in it. Do this by thinking of every moment in your life as a special gift. Refer to Chapter 8 where I presented living in the moment to help here. Make a conscious decision to put more of yourself into everything you do.

5. Never make your process of growth and the work you are doing a chore. Do something to make it more fun. Share it with someone; sing, dance, or be silly. Be passionate about your new life, your goals, and everything you are doing as you are growing.

6. Use the gift of humor. Laugh while you're re-creating yourself. It's supposed to be that way. Fun fuels internal passion.

7. Remember to be passionate about your life journey, not just the destinations and little exclamation points in it. Life is happening all around you. Embrace all of it with an unbridled passion!

 ## DRIVING IT HOME

If you're looking to increase your level of growth in your own life, be passionate about it, and continue focusing on the processes that will get you there. You are the author of this wonderful forward-life progression. Be passionate about who you are, and who you are becoming. If you do, you just may understand what "high on life" is all about.

**YOUR DECLARATION IS:** *I will feel my passion; I will feel my world!*

 ## ONWARD

As you grow in the Process Way of Life, a newfound sense of wisdom begins to enter your life. I'm going to examine this wonderful gift, and how to make it a guiding component of your new life next.

◇◇◇◇◇◇◇◇◇◇◇◇◇◇◇

# CHAPTER 28

# Wisdom, and the Arrogance/ Humility Paradigm

*Knowledge can create power for you, but knowledge with a touch of humility creates the greater wisdom, and the greater life.*

---

**PROCESSES TO EMPLOY:** Brutal Honesty, I Over E, Present/ Understand/Fix, Slowing Down Life's Pace, Dignity, Honor, Humility, Intelligent Decision-Making, Morality

---

THE TRADITIONAL DEFINITION OF WISDOM is the quality of having experience, knowledge, and good judgment; the quality of being wise. Wisdom also includes variables such as intelligence, common sense, circumspection, good sound judgment, and scholarship. This is, indeed, a very enlightened approach to living. Unfortunately, wisdom can also have its downside.

As your Process Way of Life journey continues, you can get ahead of yourself as your internal growth increases. This happens because, for the first time in your life, you are developing and using intellectual capabilities you never understood before. So, you need to learn how to use your new skills to your advantage, and for the long run. Most of the time, so long as you stay close to your processes, and keep focused on the Process Way of Life, everything proceeds smoothly.

What can happen at this stage, however, is that you experience a reduction in conflict, stress, and anxiety. At the same time, you are feeling increases in intellectual functioning and decision-making capabilities. Worldly common sense would seem to be telling you that you just might not need to depend on the processes as much as you have.

This way of thinking is like what schizophrenics who take antipsychotic medications might do. After six months or a year, they might decide that things are going very well. They have experienced a reduction in disorganized thinking, so they can stop taking the medicine. Soon thereafter, the symptoms begin to return. For them, the medicine was part of their process. When they removed that part of the process, the old symptoms began to reappear. The processes, just as they become the power, have illuminated your world with what feels like a sharp increase in wisdom. Ah, but there is a snag with this newfound wisdom. Let's look at this in more detail.

## Fool's Gold and Beyond

I'm going to talk about two types of wisdom. I call the first type of wisdom "naive wisdom" and the second type, "authentic wisdom." Naive wisdom is wisdom without an adequate foundation. It is the accumulation of new information that is misperceived as wisdom. It is newly acquired knowledge that makes a person feel wiser, but it doesn't possess enough of the life experiences and intellectual connectors to make it functional. Authentic wisdom is connected. It possesses a deeper understanding of life, connects throughout a person's physical, intellectual, emotional, and spiritual attributes, and has a strong sense of application.

Unless we are born with prophetic gifts, all of us must progress through naive wisdom to arrive at authentic wisdom. This simply means that as you are proceeding through life, you will begin to learn. As you do, you will assimilate what you are experiencing into your existing storehouse of knowledge. As this learning takes place, you begin to apply your new knowledge in your daily life. That's where all your processes come into play. All of them are designed to make you a wiser person. Initially, as you are presented with this new information, you're not sure exactly how to apply it.

The application process develops because you begin to connect the new information to your internal attributes. As this occurs, you begin to solidify the foundations for authentic wisdom. *Having authentic wisdom means that you are now connecting the information physically, intellectually, emotionally, and spiritually, in balanced fashion.* You start using a meaningful approach that is logical, intelligent, thoughtful, humble, and has a big-picture oriented, common-sense application. Before this happens, though, you may become a bit cocky, and feel that you don't need the processes as much as you did earlier in the program, and this is where your program wheels can begin to wobble. The table below gives a breakdown of the differences between authentic wisdom and naive wisdom.

## AUTHENTIC VERSUS NAIVE WISDOM

| Authentic Wisdom | Naive Wisdom |
|---|---|
| Many life experiences | Fewer life experiences |
| Based on humility | Can be arrogant |
| Loves to be the student. | Has difficulty with continued learning |
| Understands reliance on the processes | Less reliance on the processes |
| Continues to move slowly | Has accelerated pace in life |
| Sees the bigger picture | Focus on smaller circumstances |
| Life is still a journey | Sees some of the destination realized |

## Not So Fast: The Arrogance/Humility Paradigm

As you become more efficient in the application of the Process Way of Life, and start feeling stronger in it, you can become overconfident, and you might firmly believe that you are now more intelligent. You may also begin to abandon all or some of the parts of your processes. The vehicle for this to happen is another age-old enemy: arrogance. Arrogance doesn't have to be an in-your-face presentation. It doesn't have to attack, nor be condescending. It doesn't have to think it knows everything either.

There is a subtle form of arrogance that develops as your processes take hold, and you start to realize some successes in your personal growth. Say hello to *subdued arrogance*. This is a natural development, and you can expect this to occur from time to time. The trick is to catch this subtle form of egotism before it creates problems, or even worse, disasters.

You operate in a "can't see the forest for the trees" world. You are living life as you are addressing your needs there, so it can be difficult to understand when subdued arrogance makes its devilish debut. Since identifying the appearance of subdued arrogance can be difficult, it makes more sense to infuse your program with one of the more important processes. I'm talking about humility.

## Deceptively Strong

"Humility" is typically defined as modesty, meekness, and even submissiveness. For our purposes, I am describing humility as *the willingness to place yourself at the grace of your processes, always keeping yourself subservient to their design.* Remember, the processes are the power. They created the wisdom. Humility as I am defining it, keeps you connected with the power of the processes. It helps keep you balanced physically, intellectually, emotionally, and spiritually, and from getting too full of yourself, which can happen with naive wisdom. *Authentic wisdom cannot exist without humility.*

You were born with the capacity to increase and enhance your own states of wisdom, but this is an acquired capability. Also, it must be cultivated and refined routinely to reach the potential for it to guide you through life. No one can do this alone, and no part of our Process Way of Life takes more time to evolve than true wisdom.

Arrogance, and the disconnection from your processes that it instigates, can quickly cause internal imbalance. Even subdued arrogance can fool you into believing that you are more intelligent and more in control than you really are. Arrogance rarely possesses the ability to learn. It will quickly become an empty destination; a true knowledge graveyard. Continued and sustained learning is crucial to internal balance, and ultimately, to personal happiness and fulfillment.

Humility opens the door for continued personal growth, and keeps you connected with power sources which fuel your journey. Arrogance is the student who becomes the teacher, and then refuses to continue being the student. Humility is the student who, while rising to the level of teacher, always remains a student of life. No one who possesses an arrogant disposition ever acquires authentic wisdom. Wisdom on that level is reserved for those individuals who embrace the gift of studenthood. To operate on this level, you must remain humble.

 **TIME TO TAKE ACTION**

1. Remain a student of life. Love the process of being a student, and never feel as though you have learned enough. Ask questions, and always be willing to learn from others. Judicially attempt to make any changes that will help you grow, and enhance the quality of your life.

2. Understand that humility simply means that you are keeping yourself connected to your processes, and that you understand that the processes are your teachers.

3. Don't be fooled by arrogance. It feels powerful, but it is nothing more than an external representation of internal imbalance and insecurity. You will always need your processes.

4. Always keep in mind that arrogance must lead to disconnection. Humility always stays connected because it never assumes that it is larger than the processes, and the processes are life.

5. Keep this in mind: Arrogance moves swiftly; humility takes its time. Go slow and allow yourself the luxury of understanding the new approach you are employing in your life. Refer to my practical suggestions in Chapter 5 if you need help.

 **DRIVING IT HOME**

The processes provide you with what you need to aspire to the level of authentic wisdom. Humility ensures that you can stay connected to the Process Way of Life. So remain a student, stay connected to the processes, stay humble, learn to be wise, and enjoy life.

**YOUR DECLARATION IS:** *I will remain humble, so I can be wise.*

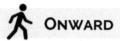 **ONWARD**

With creativity, passion, and wisdom entering your life, something wonderful is beginning to happen. You are starting to feel the processes coming alive in you. I'll show you how this happens in the next chapter.

◇◇◇◇◇◇◇◇◇◇◇◇◇

# CHAPTER 29

# Breathing Life
# Into the Processes

*You can breathe life into any process you choose to make part of yourself.*
*The life of that process will alter your existence forever.*

---

**PROCESSES TO EMPLOY**: Brutal Honesty, I Over E, Present/
Understand/Fix, Slowing Down Life's Pace, Commitment,
Internal Balance, Life's Natural Flow, Trust

---

FOR CENTURIES, MAN HAS EMPLOYED VARIOUS FORMS of tools to
assist him in his endeavors. As time progressed, the tools became
more sophisticated, and both our alliance with, and our reliance on
them, more pronounced. Our relationship with tools has assisted
us in every facet of our development, and now reaches into virtual-
information processing modalities that have expanded our capabilities into worlds which we never dreamed existed. The symbiotic
relationship between human beings and their tools has fostered
a way of life whose boundaries appear to be limitless in what has
become a colossal and spectacular human metamorphosis.

The colloquial definition of a tool is a device or implement,
especially held in one's hand, to carry out a specific function. Tools
are not limited to physical apparatuses. All the processes I've been
outlining may be defined as tools. The most important difference
between physical tools and our process tools is that physical tools do
not have independent life. Process tools, however, exist within the
confines of a constantly evolving life force.

The processes which I've been introducing are tools which will help us become happier, healthier people. They are the products of, and live in a brain which is alive and constantly redefining itself. These healthy living processes take on a life that is symbiotic with their host, always changing with it, and often introducing changes with respect to the way we think, feel, and behave. I am now beginning a pivotal chapter in the Process Way of Life. This symbiotic relationship between yourself and your processes has created an entirely new life.

As you continue to employ your new processes, they become united with your brain, and they live within you each day of your life. Your processes have become part of who you are. They are alive, and live and breathe as you do. To that end, you can never really leave the processes completely. You may choose not to focus on them, or some part of them. However, it's difficult to turn off something that become so closely and intimately connected to who you are, and to whom you have become.

## The Breath of Life

For this to occur, a process needs to be alive. This doesn't say that it has independent life. Its life more closely coincides with that of an unborn baby, whose existence is intrinsically dependent on the nutrition it receives from its mother. That fetus is alive, and is a life process developing in the womb. The fetus cannot live independently of its mother, but it certainly has life. Your processes, just like the unborn child, cannot live independently, but so long as you breath and have consciousness, they are alive.

What began as mere tools to help you overcome what was hurting you and making you unhappy has gained life in you, and influences the way you live. You are no longer simply using tools. You are drawing on resources that are connected to you; that have become naturally essential to the life you are living. The processes have become part of the natural flow of your brain.

From birth, through adolescence, spanning mature life, and into your elderly years, the brain undergoes significant physical changes.

In addition to the natural changes the brain experiences, using the processes, over time, also changes your brain. If you commit to processes which routinely tell your brain to function differently, the brain, over time, changes to accommodate the new information. As a result, those processes become part of the brain's daily life cycle. They become alive in you.

The processes start as consciously applied. That is, you must routinely infuse them with conscious energy, since even though they have always been part of you, they were not always included in your natural routine. Over time, with continued focus on the processes, your brain adjusts, and the processes become more automatic. As this happens, your brain integrates the new process into your existing internal framework, and what were two distinct life functions become one.

## May the (Life) Force Be with You

Something that began as a simple tool to help you change the way you were living has evolved into a process-charged life force. Thus, the processes become who you are. This is one of the most important long-term goals of our program. As you continue to feed your brain with process-infused energy, your brain adjusts, and eventually those processes become your standard way of living. The processes have been given life through their attachment to a brain which is alive and structurally changing to accommodate them. Together, they have created a new and dynamic life force: you. Here's how it happened:

➤ You understood that you needed help.

➤ You searched for a way to make that happen.

➤ You found the Process Way of Life.

➤ You decided to use the program to help you change your life.

➤ You started with the first four bookend processes: Brutal Honesty, I Over E, Present/Understand/Fix, Slowing Down Life's Pace.

- Seeing them begin to work, you made a decision to use the entire program.

- You stayed committed, accepted the advice given to you, and didn't give up.

- You began to trust the processes, and as a result, yourself.

- You begin using the Process Way of Life as your natural way to live.

- The Process Way of Life has become who you are. It is alive in you.

Everything you think about and do has life, and those thoughts and behaviors, which you choose to nurture with the gifts of time and commitment, can become permanent. You then, are breathing extended, and eventually, permanent life into them. So, if you are willing to give the Process Way of Life time to grow, it will not only be a program that will change your life, it will become alive in you, and it will become who you are.

I've talked about the natural flow of things in our lives. The permanent change that comes with continued focus on a process over a significant amount of time produces a natural change, one that the brain willingly accepts, and one that can radically change the way you live. It can only operate at this level if it attaches itself to a life force; your life force. When it does, it becomes alive, and as it lives, growth occurs, and continues to evolve. It will alter your existence, forever. Remember, the life force has always been in you. Stay committed! Make two become one!

## ⏱ Time To Take Action

1. Use the processes every day. Never stop doing so.

2. The more often the processes are used, the greater impact you will realize regarding your personal growth. Use them every day, and to their maximum potential.

3. Since the processes lead to internal balance, trust them. Give the processes the time they need to become a natural part of the way you live life. This will provide them with time they need to come alive in you.

4. Never abandon the processes, even when you become happy with the results. The processes have become part of your life. With continued use, the life of the processes will become stronger, providing new growth, over-and-over again. It is a marvelous, never-ending reciprocal relationship; a true journey changer.

##  Driving It Home

What began as a process to help you change your life has become an entirely new life. Now, you can understand why life is a journey. There is no destination. The journey is the destination. Give your new journey life by giving it time. Through your new living relationship with the processes, you will learn to realize the power you always had.

**YOUR DECLARATION IS:** *The processes and I are one, and we will stay that way.*

## ✺ ONWARD

You have come far in your Process Way of Life. It's so important to be thankful for all you have been given, and the new person you are becoming. The next chapter opens the beginning of the second set of the Process Way of Life process bookends. They are: Gratitude: The Great Connector, Chapter 30; In-Service: Understanding Who You Are By Serving Others, Chapter 31; and Opening Your Mind: Embracing Your Limitlessness—The Power of Faith, Chapter 32. They will introduce you to a finer understanding of internal balance, and the pure love it creates. On to Gratitude.

◇◇◇◇◇◇◇◇◇◇◇◇◇

# Gratitude:
# The Great Connector

*Let gratitude be the bridge between what you thought was not,*
*and what can be.*

---

**PROCESSES TO EMPLOY:** Brutal Honesty, I Over E, Present/
Understand/Fix, Slowing Down Life's Pace, Gratitude, Humility,
Keeping Life Simple, Life on Life's Terms, Living in the Moment,
Patience, Trust

---

YOU HAVE ARRIVED AT A DEFINING POINT of the Process Way of
Life; a process that can bridge the gap between where you started,
and where you are going. That process is gratitude. Gratitude
has been defined as the quality of being thankful, appreciative, or
beholden. It helps you to understand the graces and gifts which have
been bestowed on you, helps you appreciate the little things in life,
and lets others know that you are not taking them for granted.

When it comes to being a good person, gratitude is something
you want in your process toolbox. Most of us are grateful for those
people, possessions, and events in our lives, some of which are happening, and others which have already occurred. This is what we
might call *retroactive gratitude*. We are expressing our thankfulness,
albeit it after the fact.

In this chapter, I am focusing on a different type of gratitude,
a process I refer to as *proactive global gratitude* (proactive because it

is self-initiating; global because it attaches itself to everything). As opposed to being an expression of thankfulness and appreciation for something we have already experienced, proactive global gratitude does not require a person, place, or wonderful event to be expressed.

Retroactive gratitude waits for something to be grateful for, while proactive gratitude seeks out something to be grateful for. In typical retroactive gratitude, something occurs, and then we respond. In proactive global gratitude, there is no triggering event, or special deed performed by another person. It occurs because we are making a conscious effort to be grateful for all the moments of our life. It's a process that is constantly operating, so what occurs in the external world is received, and absorbed internally, finding its way into an environment which is already steeped in gratitude. The following table shows the difference between retroactive and proactive global gratitude.

## RETROACTIVE VERSUS PROACTIVE GLOBAL GRATITUDE

| RETROACTIVE GRATITUDE | PROACTIVE GLOBAL GRATITUDE |
|---|---|
| Reacts to something good | Always active internally |
| Is short-lived | Never turns off |
| Appreciates specific moments | Appreciates every moment |
| Responds to new external stimuli | Self-generating; excitement not needed |
| Always comes from the outside | Born and lives on the inside |
| Comes from external events | Comes from internal processes |
| Experiences gratitude interrupts | No gratitude interruptions |
| Waits for something to be thankful for | Seeks out something to be grateful for |

# Magnetic Personality

*Proactive global gratitude is a positive internal state that is always operating, and attaches itself to every part of life.* External events are channeled to a positively charged, gratitude-infused repository that is always ready to receive them. It needs nothing from the external world to ignite it. You can be grateful when you get what you want. There is no power in that, and the energy source is short-lived. However, those of you who elect to attach gratitude to every part of your journey, invite a new energy source into your life which binds your processes with all that lives, and all that is. The following example illustrates the distinction between retroactive gratitude and proactive global gratitude.

## THE GRATEFUL GIRLS

Erin and Tammy just graduated from high school. Both are preparing to apply to local colleges. Erin, the oldest of three children, loves spending time with people. Tammy is an athlete. She's a fun-loving person who is always outgoing and helpful to others.

Erin and Tammy are seen by those who know them as very nice people who are always respectful to others, and are always pleasant and accommodating. It doesn't seem to take much to please either girl, and both are quick to express their gratitude for even the smallest of favors.

There seems to be something just a bit different, however, in the way Erin expresses herself. Though Tammy is always thankful regarding what she has received in her life, Erin seems to be grateful all the time. She doesn't need something to be thankful for. Her general demeanor lets others know how grateful she is, not just about what happened, or the gifts that she receives, but about every moment in her life. In fact, even without expressing her gratitude, it seems to come out in everything she says and does. This quality rubs off on others in her life, and they tend to reciprocate by being a bit more grateful when they are with her.

To examine one of the more important differences between proactive global gratitude and retroactive gratitude, let's, once again, consider the destination-versus-journey paradigm. Retroactive gratitude is expressed when you reach a destination. Something occurs, or someone does something nice for you. When this happens, you become grateful. You are thankful, and you may express your gratitude to another person.

Another form of retroactive gratitude is when you work hard to achieve something, and at the end of your hard work you are rewarded. You express gratitude because you have been blessed with something that you have been working hard to attain. In each of these cases, you arrived at a destination. Something changed in your life, and you are grateful to receive it.

Proactive global gratitude is part of the journey. Like all the processes which feed your balanced attributes, it is expressed throughout your journey, regardless of the size of the payoff, and even when there is no payoff at all. You are consciously attempting to be grateful for every moment of your life.

Since proactive global gratitude needs no destination, you introduce it routinely. In addition, proactive global gratitude avoids "gratitude interrupts." These are times when you are not feeling grateful, and may become anxious about what you don't have. These interrupts can have a profound impact on your internal balance.

Anything that is positive carries with it a positive source of energy. When being grateful is a way of life, your energy stays positive, always moving out from the inside. You want your internal influence over that external territory to always be the primary way you navigate through your life. Proactive global gratitude does just that.

This doesn't mean that retroactive gratitude is not positive. You should always be grateful for the gifts and graces you receive. You should also freely express your gratitude to those who were kind enough to think about you. What I am talking about here though, is developing yet one more tool that you will routinely use to bring positive energy into your life.

# The Advanced Scout, and the Grateful Journey

When gratitude exists routinely inside of you, it performs as an advanced scout, moving outward, and redefining everything that touches you. Not only can it appreciate positive energy, it possesses the ability to transform negative energy into a positive energy source. Proactive global gratitude, if it is part of your routine life journey, and being expressed moment by moment in your life, is a defense which reduces the potential for negative charges to impact your life. So, how do you move from a destination type of gratitude, to gratitude that is journey-oriented?

You are going to consciously train yourself to rethink the way you interact with your environment. In Chapter 6, I discussed how everything you do is a process, even something as simple as brushing your teeth. In that chapter, I broke that activity into its smaller process features, as I examined all the smaller component features that are involved in the creation of the little endeavors in your life. There are many.

Try to do this for all the little parts of your life. Break every little endeavor down into the little process, those seemingly minute moments, that are involved in it. Be grateful for all of them, and for now, consciously keep that process going. Identify all the little positives, intellectually tell yourself how wonderful they are, and mark that territory, just as we did in Chapter 8. As with all our processes, given the gift of time and commitment, you will begin to see proactive global gratitude become part of your life.

You start this way to alter the way you think, from *retroactive gratitude* to *proactive global gratitude*. Make a conscious effort to attach gratitude to everything that you see, hear, feel, and do. When you do, you will be surprised at how much there is to be grateful for.

Gratitude in destination form is short-lived. This runs counter to everything that I am teaching. You're not looking for quick fixes, and you're not looking for anything in your Process Way of Life to be temporary. You want growth that is sustained; growth that will survive the test of time. That comes from the inside. So, feel your gratitude from the inside, and express it as often as you can, for everything.

You are evolving from simple retroactive, or destination-oriented gratitude toward a moment-by-moment understanding of the quality of your life, and the positive energy that resides there. You are taking destination-oriented gratitude, which emanates from outside of yourself, consciously moving it into a journey-oriented internal state, and using it to influence the way you perceive your entire environment.

Gratitude has indeed become the bridge between what you thought was not, and what can be. You can, routinely, throughout your day, call upon this energy, and apply it to every circumstance in your life. The internal balance between your physical, intellectual, emotional, and spiritual talents will soar. The more positive energy that can be applied to these attributes, the more efficient, fulfilled, and happy you will become. Rejoice in what you have and who you are, always. Your life on the inside is turning a wonderful corner. Be grateful for all of it, all the time!

 **TIME TO TAKE ACTION**

1. Make a list of everything and everyone in your life you are grateful for. There will be many. Break them down into the little parts, and be grateful for all of them.

2. Identify a positive characteristic associated with everything you see, feel, touch, and hear. Do this for the people in your life as well. Simply be thankful that you and they exist.

3. Work to incorporate gratitude into your "in the moment" way of doing things. By slowing down the pace of your life, as I presented in Chapter 5, and consciously paying attention to all the little processes happening around you, you can identify even the smallest gifts that can be so special to you. Moment by moment is where gratitude lives best.

 ## Driving It Home

Gratitude must exist with every breath you take to keep the positive flow of energy uninterrupted. Gratitude will help you remove boundaries and limitations that can impair your movement to higher states of consciousness and emotional fulfillment. Internally thriving, always in the moment, proactive global gratitude unites you more efficiently with life's natural flow, and on the grand scale, with the universe.

**YOUR DECLARATION IS:** *I will stay grateful; I will be connected to everything; I will be limitless.*

 ## Onward

So that you may enhance your connection with others, and turn the gains you are making into a personal world-changing and loving enterprise, you must always be in service of others. Giving multiplies your gains, and connects you with your spirituality. I'll explain this process in the next chapter.

◇◇◇◇◇◇◇◇◇◇◇◇◇◇

# CHAPTER 31

# Understanding Who You Are by Serving Others

*Only through sincere and dedicated service to others can you understand who you are, and why you are here.*

**PROCESSES TO EMPLOY:** Brutal Honesty, I Over E, Present/ Understand/Fix, Slowing Down Life's Pace, Being in Service, Dignity, Honor, Humility, Internal Focus, Trust

IN THIS EYE-FOR-AN-EYE, LIVE-FOR-YOURSELF WORLD, it's easy to lose perspective of how important it is to help others. As you continue to progress in the Process Way of Life, it is important to share your new gifts. The blessings associated with helping others can become life-changing events for you. Your life with others is best lived as a reciprocal journey. Giving completes your own circle of growth, while it also enriches the lives of those you touch.

Humans are social beings, and we learn from each other as we evolve. Learning is a reciprocal process where one partner assumes the role of teacher, while the other acts as the student. Teaching and learning, though, occur simultaneously for both the teacher and the student. Though one may assume the guiding role as teacher, there is always something for the teacher to learn from the student. With this concept in mind, I am presenting the process of being in-service to others.

While one person is acting as the helper, and the other the

recipient of the service, it's far more complex than that, and in each case, the reciprocal process is always in play. When you are giving to another person, though that person may be incapable of returning the favor, you are also receiving. Some of what you receive may be in the form of the gratitude the other person may express, while the greater portion comes from the growth which occurs within you.

## Maximum Freebie

Being in service to others, as the Process Way of Life teaches, means *to help them address their needs as they express them, without receiving or asking to receive either payback or attention from others for our actions.* When you give to others and expect to be paid back, you are already receiving your reward. There is little, if any, internal growth associated with service for attention.

Something that rewards you externally minimizes the amount of internal growth you will experience. If you are looking for a payback, or some type of notoriety for your actions, your motivation for service was not as much to be purely altruistic, but instead, to be seen in the helper role. That is not the Process Way of Life's definition of being in service.

Being in service of others, when it is a genuine motivation, comes from deep inside yourself, and has more to do with your need to share what you have with other individuals, or help them fulfill some need which they may have. Giving then, is not so much an intellectual or emotional experience. *True giving comes from the spiritual part of you, which is incapable of receiving worldly paybacks.* This statement lies at the heart of our current discourse.

There are times where the human ego wants to be seen and understood as doing the right thing. For example, someone may be trying to help a friend in need, and would like others to know that they are helping the person, not only for notoriety, but to be understood as a good person. Whereas it is good to be giving in this regard, you are still attempting to feed your ego. You want your giving to be without payback. It comes from inside you, and it is given freely. Let's look at an example to illustrate this position.

## THE GOOD DEED

Billy is in sixth grade, and is an exceptional student in school. He is quiet, thoughtful, and loves to help other people. Billy, having been taught from an early age that being in service of others is the right way to live, helps a senior citizen carry groceries from the local market to her home. The walk is about a quarter mile.

Upon returning home, he quickly tells his father about the good deed that he has done. His father simply nods his head. Once again, Billy tells his father about the deed. Once again, his father nods. As the boy begins his dissertation for the third time, his father stops him and says that he is proud of him, but that the boy needs to keep in mind that what he did is something that he should do, and that he should never expect to be commended for it.

Billy, just beginning the process of serving others, needed his father's reinforcement to feel good about what he did. He knew he was doing the right thing, but external support seemed necessary. As you grow, you want to move away from this earlier stage of giving, and understand that true giving cannot expect payback. In fact, payback negates the internal growth that comes from true altruistic gestures.

Almost everyone wants to be thought of as a good person. Doing good deeds for other people can support your ego, and that, being part of your intellectual attribute, helps you to feel good about yourself. This process, however, is very much like a quick fix. You do something, you feel good about it, and then relatively soon, that feeling wears off. Now, you must perform some other good deed, in public, so that you may feel good about yourself, once again. This is not giving from the spiritual part of yourself. Giving from your spirit does not need external support. When you are giving spiritually, you are giving without notoriety or expectation of payment. You are not giving to receive. That concept is not necessary anymore.

Service to others provides positive energy to your four internal attributes, further enhancing your internal balance, and subsequently your inner growth.

➤ Physically, giving has a calming effect on the body. Giving helps us to feel what others feel, removing us from the rapid pull of the external world.

➤ Intellectually, the process of giving without expectation of payback creates new intellectual growth independent of external sources.

➤ Emotionally, giving without expectation of payback helps remove the emotional need for instant gratification and quick fixes.

➤ Spiritually, since giving comes from our spirit, it begins a wonderful process of deep spiritual nurturance that will pave the way for the more advanced processes.

As you move into a state of internal balance, you will be giving from your spirit, and that is enough. No other payback measures up.

## The Crux of the Matter

Paybacks at the spiritual level of functioning are irrelevant, and have no meaning whatsoever. In fact, they will do little more than detract from an energy source that has become so pure and alive. To give freely is the result of a dynamic connection with another person, with the connection being the sole purpose of the action. The deeper the connection, the less need for payback.

All the growth in the world, all the balance in the world, and everything you do to become as productive and as fulfilled as you can be, have minimal value, and absolutely no way of surviving, *unless they are turned into the service of other human beings.* That service must be altruistic, with no focus on payback or notoriety, whose only purpose is to enhance the life of someone else.

At that point, you will have moved your focus away from your own needs and desires, and you will have learned to understand the bond you share with others who occupy this planet with you. This loving, altruistic bond is yet one more expression of your magnificent human journey. Understand that as life is a journey, pure altruistic giving represents one of the hallmarks of that journey. It is a compassionate expression of the loving person you are becoming.

As far back as Chapter 1, I have discussed alleviating negativity, and learning to like and eventually love who you are. Part of that process must include giving back. You accomplish this by taking the gifts which you have received as part of your Process Way of Life, and extending them outward to others. Being in service of others turns your growth outward where you can see it come alive in others.

Also, and of most importance, you are evolving to the point of being a giving person. When you can make a statement that says you are willing to give away everything that you have gained so that another person can be fulfilled, you are becoming a person who is demonstrating pure love, as you shall soon see. The teacher nourishes the student, and the student returns the favor. So it is, as the giver nourishes the receiver, and the favor is returned.

 **TIME TO TAKE ACTION**

1. Always give unconditionally, completely, and anonymously. Never expect payback, and never let anyone know that you are giving.

2. Remember, we use our processes every day. That's how they become alive in us. Give freely every day. Love from your spirit, which cannot accept payback.

3. Be willing to share each and every gift you have attained. Understand that you gain to give back. This keeps the circle of your life energy alive, and that is why you are here.

4. Make a concerted effort to understand other people's feelings by putting yourself in their place, and give in accordance with their needs.

5. Slow down enough to be able to see that others are in need, and how you can help them. Then give because you want to give, not because you're supposed to. Remain humble; understand giving as the gift it is, and enjoy this wonderful life treasure.

 ## Driving It Home

Giving without notoriety or the expectation of a payback is higher-order living at its best. It truly does help you understand who you are and why you are here. It is so wonderful to realize that you have evolved beyond the need to gratify yourself. The moment you realize that you do not require this anymore, internal freedom takes on an entirely new definition. Being in service of others will connect you with the whole of humanity, and that is how you were meant to live.

**YOUR DECLARATION IS:** *I will serve others; I will feed my soul.*

 ## Onward

Humility, gratitude, wisdom, and being in service—these pave the way for the connection to a power much greater than ourselves. In the next chapter, I will be exploring the process of faith, and how to incorporate this magnificent treasure into your life journey.

# CHAPTER 32

# Opening Your Mind: Embracing Your Limitlessness

## The Power of Faith

*Faith is that ghost of a virtue; undefined and misaligned. When it becomes part of you, your world becomes defined and aligned forever!*

**PROCESSES TO EMPLOY:** Brutal Honesty, I Over E, Present/Understand/Fix, Slowing Down Life's Pace, Belief, Commitment, Dignity, Faith, Honor, Internal Focus, Risk-Taking

FOR MANY OF US, FAITH IS THE MOST ELUSIVE and misunderstood of all the human enterprises. Faith demands complete trust in someone or something. This pinnacle of the human spirit commands that you blindly trust in a construct that you did not devise, and that you have absolutely no control over. Humans like control, and we detest having to surrender our will to anything or anyone, especially when we can't understand all we think we need to know about it.

Faith is unconditional, and it is absolute. There is no leeway in faith. You either have all of it, or you have none of it, and this is the other stumbling block with this ghost of a virtue. We would like to kind of have faith. We like a little wiggle room in our life stage. All or nothing seems like an unsympathetic and demanding taskmaster. Traditionally, faith is a firm belief in something for which there is no proof. It is something that is believed, especially with strong conviction; often a system of spiritual beliefs. I'm presenting faith a bit differently.

*Faith is the conscious surrender of the will, which leads to absolute and unconditional trust in an entity that may or may not be proven.* The emphasis on faith in the Process Way of Life centers on the concept of *conscious surrender.* This means that you will be purposefully acquiescing or submitting yourself to someone or something.

Typically, we look at faith as something that is directed toward an unproven postulate. This is faith at the highest level. I'll discuss that as we proceed. Faith, as it begins to develop in all of us, starts with surrender to some person or entity. The surrender is a conscious decision—that is, we deliberately decide to have faith in someone or something.

It's important to understand that faith does not have to be directed at someone or something that is unknown or undefined. Faith is typically a developmental process that begins with sublimation to a concrete entity, something we know or are familiar with, such as another person, or a way of doing things. From there, it can evolve into a dynamic process that embraces the unknown and undefined, such as faith in a higher power. So, faith starts with people and events in your everyday life, which can evolve into a surrender to the more abstract entities.

## To See and Not to See

I am going to be discussing two types of faith. The first type is *concrete faith.* That, as the title suggests, is *faith in something that you can see, touch, hear, feel, and, for the most part, define.* It might be faith in your spouse, or in something that helps you in your daily functioning like the car starting or the lights turning on when you flip the switch. You give faith a chance to exist simply because you are willing to apply your energy there. By repeating this process, you trust that it will be there, and how to incorporate it in your life.

The second type of faith is abstract faith. Abstract thought is the pinnacle of all human existence. It is a type of thinking that can embrace the more undefined and cosmic levels of thought. *Abstract thought is what separates humans from other members of the animal kingdom.* I will define abstract faith shortly. To progress to the level of abstract faith, you must gain a level of proficiency regarding concrete faith. The chart illustrates the differences.

## CONCRETE FAITH AND ABSTRACT FAITH

| CONCRETE FAITH | ABSTRACT FAITH |
| --- | --- |
| Can be seen, felt, or heard | No physical substance |
| Can be easily defined | Not always easily defined |
| More human control | Less human control |
| Parameters are concrete | Parameters are abstract |
| Little intellectual expansion | Demands intellectual expansion |
| Has physical limits | Transcends physical limits |
| Faith in higher power not needed | Higher power; important parameter |

As you can see, you have considerably more control over concrete faith. The evolution from concrete to abstract faith mirrors that of primary and abstract creativity, which I discussed in Chapter 26. Before you can attain the level of abstract creativity, you must navigate through the boundaries of primary creativity. It's the same with faith. Before you can ascend to the level of abstract faith, you must transcend the boundaries of concrete faith. This progression allows you to trust the faith transition in piecemeal fashion, as it opens your mind to higher-order thought.

One of the most important features of concrete faith is the concept of committed repetition. To understand this concept, let's talk about having faith in our processes. I have discussed how commitment to those processes eventually evolved into having faith in them, which produced personal gains, and helped you continue to use them. Notice that the key dynamic here is the concept of commitment. Commitment by its very nature stresses repetition of thought and action over time. Nothing enduring happens quickly, and repetition provides the possesses with the potential to evolve. You have been doing this with the Process Way of Life. Here's how:

➤ You committed to the Process Way of Life over a significant amount of time. That included repeating thoughts and behaviors to reinforce the changes that were occurring.

➤ As this happened, you began to see successes, some of them small, some of them a bit more elaborate.

➤ As this process unfolded, you began to trust what you were doing.

➤ You began to expect positive results, because the Process Way of Life is working for you, and you began to believe in it, that is, to trust it.

➤ Your trust, then, began to develop into a sense of concrete faith.

➤ You know the process works, that is, it helps you grow and feel good.

➤ You have developed the faith that it will continue to support you in this concrete fashion.

So, concrete faith is the commitment to a process that must occur over a significant amount of time, and must include repeating the necessary thoughts and behaviors to reinforce the changes that are occurring.

## Leap of Faith

I have discussed how the Process Way of Life, which you have embraced and committed to over time, became part of who you are. I have also stressed how everything you need is already inside you. You simply need to access and develop it. Faith has always been one of your internal processes. It has the same properties as the rest of your processes. You are merely developing something you already have.

Since the Process Way of Life has become who you are, faith in it also begins to become part of who you are. Remember, the processes are alive in you. Faith, being one of your processes, is no exception. You already know that the program works, and now you know you have faith in it. This means that you are trusting it unconditionally. Now, you consciously begin to understand that you have faith; that you are using it as a process. Just as the other processes gained life in you as you committed yourself to them, faith is now alive in you.

Though you may not be aware of what is occurring, you are beginning to open your mind to the potentiality of abstract faith, that is, the ability to have faith in something that is without physical or logical parameters. You may not understand this, but something is changing. This evolution to the beginning of abstract faith gained life because you committed yourself to it, and nurtured it with the gift of time at the concrete level. You have opened yet another process door.

The concept of faith is typically associated with spirituality, and with God. Whereas faith and God are inseparable, they do not exist together until you make a conscious decision to connect them. Before one takes the concept of any higher power into one's heart, one must be a person who can put their faith in something. My goal in this part of the discussion is not to attempt to sway you toward the concept of God. That will be an individual choice; however, putting yourself in a position to acquire abstract faith is preparing yourself for human evolution at its absolute apex.

*Abstract faith is the ability to understand that something greater than you exists, and that by defining that power, acquiescing to it, and embracing it, you become part of that power source.* Earlier in our presentation, I began to talk about the various processes which would move you to a more efficient and fulfilling way of living life. You gave those processes an opportunity to work, defined and embraced them, stayed committed to them, began to have faith in them, and are now reaping their benefits. By doing so, you tapped into energy sources, which have moved you into more powerful positions as you live life. Logically then, if you become a person of faith, and move your capabilities toward embracing faith into the abstract realms, you can also be embracing the energy sources which exist at those levels.

So, the question isn't whether or not you choose to apply faith to God. The question is whether or not you're willing to open your mind to becoming a person of abstract faith. Are you willing to make the attempt to direct your energies to a powerful and dynamic process that might be undefined, unknown, and beyond the reach of your physical senses? Ask yourself these questions:

1. Am I willing to open my mind enough to understand what faith at the abstract level is all about?

2. Am I willing to give myself the opportunity to work with abstract faith as I did with my other processes?

3. Am I willing to take the risk and continue to grow, or am I going to call it quits here?

4. Am I satisfied with the concrete level of growth I have made, or am I willing to take a risk beyond my tangible safe place, and into the realms of abstract faith, the highest-order process of all?

## Oh, My God!

So many people have struggled with the concept of faith, because they have made a premature decision to not embrace the concept of God. Rarely does the concept of God precede our ability to be people of faith. It's no wonder why so many people struggle with their faith. Embracing abstract faith opens the mind to the potential to evolve to a point where it can wrap itself around the concept of trusting an unknown energy source. The keyword is *trust*. Faith demands trust. This doesn't mean that you merely accept the possibility of some higher energy source. It means that you are willing to open your mind to defining and trying something new, just as you did with our other processes. You didn't trust them when you started the Process Way of Life either.

When you began your new journey, you didn't understand, let alone have any faith in the Process Way of Life. You knew nothing about it, and you were content to blame everyone and everything for the problems in your life. As you worked with the program, stayed consistent, opened your mind to its potentialities, and began to trust it, you started to reap the benefits. What in the world would make you think you can't do this at a higher level?

You've already proven that you can have faith in a life program. You never even remotely considered the possibility before you began your Process Way of Life. At that time, even concrete faith was an abstract concept to you. You are in the same position now. You are coming face-to-face with the next step in the program. Your decision to attach your faith to God is your own, but make that decision after you understand what abstract faith is.

You start to give faith a chance to exist in an abstract state by simply opening your mind to the possibility that an energy source beyond your definition exists. However, as you saw in the development of our Process Way of Life, you must then make attempts to *define* what that process is, and how that abstract process can work for you. It's not enough to simply throw caution to the wind and say something bigger than myself exists, but I don't know what it is, and I'm not concerned about it. That's a cop out, and it has nothing to do with faith, or personal growth, for that matter. You are no longer a cop-out person. You are a definition person. You don't run from what you don't understand. You face it head-on, define it, and come to terms with it. It's just another process.

So, the process begins by opening your mind to the potential of abstract faith. Then, as you saw when you began using the Process Way of Life, you begin to define what the process looks like. It's Present/Understand/Fix all over again. You define anything by opening your mind to new possibilities and new potentialities. You want to more comprehensively examine those undefined parameters to see if and how they might be incorporated into your life.

Never close your mind to any possibility. As soon as you do, your growth comes to an end. If you don't attempt to define and embrace the possibility of abstract faith, you remain lodged at the level of concrete faith, and your personal growth will coincide with that choice. Remember our old nemesis arrogance, and how it stopped the learning process? Have a little humility here. Open your mind and explore a process that can raise you to new heights, and a limitless existence.

Are you going to remain in your concrete faith safe zones, or are you going to challenge yourself and see what abstract faith can offer? Growth always includes some degree of risk. Step out of your comfort zone once again, and see what life at this level might offer you. What do you have to lose? Don't decide that you can't be a person of faith, just because you don't like the G word.

If you have become committed to your processes, you know they work, and you know that your faith in them has changed your life. You took a risk when you decided to make them part of your life. Don't stop the process now. Open your mind to see what abstract faith can do for you. Then, define your abstract faith.

You define abstract faith the same way you did with every other process. You use the Present/Understand/Fix formula.

1. You present what you want to do. In this case, you want to examine the possibility of including abstract faith in your process toolbox.

2. You take the necessary steps to gather as much information as you possibly can about the subject.

3. You remove all preconceived notions about abstract faith from your information gathering process.

4. You go slow and you put your intellect before your emotions. You are looking for facts, and information that can lead you to a conclusion.

5. You open your mind, remain unbiased, and follow the information.

6. You give yourself the opportunity to try something new, even if you're not sure about what to do with it. Movement to the higher order of human existence consistently raises the bar when it comes to opening your mind to accept new information.

7. You accept and attempt to use the new information, even if it runs counter to the way you hoped things would turn out.

This process will be more demanding than the others. For the first time in the Process Way of Life, you're being asked to wrap yourself around something you can't see, touch, or, for that matter, use your senses to understand. It's growth at an entirely new level.

As you proceeded in the Process Way of Life, the processes added definition where little previously existed. The results have been life-changing. Take the risk. Add more definition. It will take time, but you are worth it. This is the pinnacle of human existence, and the payoff will be commensurate with the effort. Do you really want to limit yourself to the concrete boundaries and the limitations of a finite mind? Take another risk. S-T-R-E-T-C-H! The Process Way of Life never stops. As you proceed with anything in life, the higher levels of evolution require greater risks, and more commitment. The payoffs at this level though are astronomical.

 ## TIME TO TAKE ACTION

1. Faith begins by staying committed to a successful concrete program over time. Use the Present/Understand/Fix process to examine the information.

2. As with any process, get all the information. Read as much as you can. Talk to others who have abstract faith. Do your homework on this one.

3. Stop being afraid of the G word. Get out of your safe place. Even process-oriented growth can create safe places. Ask yourself how fulfilled you want to become.

4. Rid your mind of your preconceived notions. Preconceived information contaminates the information-gathering process.

5. Don't make up your mind about how far you're willing to go on this one before you examine the information. Don't put your abstract cart before your process horse.

6. Begin to define your faith. Stay away from cop outs like "I know there's something bigger out there, but I don't know what it is, and I'm not concerned about it." You're better than that. Define your abstract faith just like you did with every other process.

7. Find out what the next step in your own personal evolution can offer through an honest effort to include your new information into your life. Life is a journey. Treat this as part of it, and push past your perceived limitations.

 ## DRIVING IT HOME

Nothing can reduce fear and uncertainty from our lives better than faith. Even with your faith at a concrete level, you are capable of thinking, feeling, and behaving in ways that you never assumed possible. Imagine what the possibilities could be if you allow yourself to evolve into abstract faith. Indeed, you will possess the ability to overcome everything.

**YOUR DECLARATION IS**: *I will have faith, I will fear nothing, I can overcome anything.*

 ## ONWARD

Humility, gratitude, wisdom, being in service of others, and faith have brought you to the culmination of the Process Way of Life. The stage is set. This is where the internal balance you have worked so hard for meets pure love.

# CHAPTER 33

# In the Name of Love

## INTERNAL BALANCE COMES ALIVE

*Internal balance is the finely tuned machine that opens the door to self-love. Do everything in your life with love, and watch your world come alive.*

---

**PROCESSES TO EMPLOY:** Brutal Honesty, I Over E, Present/ Understand/Fix, Slowing Down Life's Pace, Dignity, Faith, Gratitude, Humility, In Service, Internal Balance, Internal Focus, Trust, Wisdom

---

IT COULD BE ONE OF THE MOST ASKED QUESTIONS in the modern world. What is love? Most people would say that it's an emotion; an affair of the heart. It's the most important of all human emotions, and the most misunderstood. Momentarily, I'll be submitting a different explanation, as I define this transcendent paragon of the human spirit. My purpose in both this chapter and Chapter 34 is to provide you with a logical definition of love, an in-depth analysis of the important information to understand it, and a practical way to apply it in your life.

Let's look at human life as a pyramid.

➤ On the bottom, we find the foundation: our physical life, which is represented by all the bodily functions that sustain us.

- One level up from our physical existence is where our emotions reside. This is where all our feelings, positive and negative, live. Though not as primal as our physicality, emotions are quick, and closely connected to our primal instincts.

- One level above our emotions, we find our intellect, which allows us to rationally and reasonably move through our environment, providing us with the capabilities of productive decision-making and deductive reasoning.

- In the level above intellect comes spirituality. That is where love, in its purest sense, resides.

- As you will learn, being balanced internally sets the stage for all the love you will need, and the exciting potential to extend your balanced form of love outward.

## Same Old Love Song

If you can't love yourself, it's next to impossible to love someone else. Most of you have heard this overused cliché. The problem is that each time some expert tells you about loving yourself, what's typically lacking is how to develop the ability to understand what love is. It's one thing to say you love yourself, but one must understand what love is to make this happen. Though parts of love do include treating other people as you would have them treat you, loving yourself, allowing yourself to be loved, and spreading love throughout the world—these, rather than defining love, are actions we perform because we love.

You need to move yourself away from the notion that love is something that you do, receive, or even feel. That's not to say that these actions don't occur when love is part of your life. It simply says that it's missing the biggest part of the picture. Pure love—that is, love that is spiritual—is a direct by-product of internal balance. It is a constant internal state, always operating within you. This will become clear as we proceed.

The following table illustrates the differences between worldly love and pure love.

## WORLDLY LOVE VERSUS PURE LOVE

| WORLDLY LOVE | PURE LOVE |
|---|---|
| Product of internal imbalance | Product of internal balance |
| Searched for outside of you | Born inside you |
| Needs excitement | Based on tranquility |
| Is emotional | Is spiritual |
| Dependent, needs outside reinforcement | Independent, not needing reinforcement |
| Has frequent ups and down | Is stable and peaceful |
| Uses internal energy | Creates internal energy |

In the Process Way of Life, "pure love" is a state when *one's physical, intellectual, emotional, and spiritual attributes exist in balance, when worldly desires are diminished, and internal peace is realized.* In its truest form, it is serenity. It is alive, passionate, humble, grateful, wise, giving, content, and positive. We are so closely tied to our worldly needs and desires that they may interfere with our focus on internal balance. Thus, the balance needed to attain pure love is routinely challenged, but by no means impossible to attain.

## The Search for Nirvana

Throughout the annals of human experience, the quest for nirvana has captivated human imagination. Nirvana can be described as a transcendent state void of suffering, desire, and sense of self. In Buddhist philosophy, it represents the final goal that all students aspire to reach. Now, for our purposes, let's look at nirvana as a state when the entire human organism operates in balance, reducing worldly desires, and enhancing peace and tranquility throughout the body, mind, and spirit. Whether we are talking about nirvana or internal balance, both possess the same common goal, that being internal peace.

When I refer to the Process Way of Life definition of love, I am talking about an internal balance which creates a complete sense of peace. Pure love is the state of internal peace, which comes from internal balance, which is the final byproduct of the Process Way of Life. Internal balance produces a pure, tranquil, but powerful form of energy. That pure energy is what I am calling love. Think of all the growth you have been making by using your processes. The goal has always been internal balance. Pure love needs internal balance to exist. To love yourself means to be in a state of internal balance, where your physical, intellectual, emotional, and spiritual attributes operate in unison. It is the point where internal conflicts are minimized, and you feel balanced and at peace with yourself. You feel love.

## Love, Pure and Simple

I discussed how your processes come alive in Chapter 29. Staying committed and developing your processes leads to internal balance. Internal balance is alive. So, love is a product of a process-induced balanced internal state that is alive and becomes pure energy. It produces an energy source which is alive and vibrant. That energy source is vital, dynamic, and passionate. It wraps itself around everything it touches as it permeates all aspects of your life.

Love then, is not a feeling. It is not a function of the heart. It's imperative that you move on from that misleading, greeting-card way that incorrectly defines the most important attribute of the human spirit. Love comes from our willingness to adopt and maintain processes that lead to internal growth and, finally, to internal balance. When this occurs, you will understand love, you will feel love, you will know how to love, and you will know how to receive love. Everything you will do becomes a function of an energy source which is alive, balanced, and is now able to embrace life. It does this peacefully and lovingly. It allows you to use that energy to love yourself, and others.

The components of internal-balance based pure love are:

➤ The understanding that the capacity to love has always been inside you, and can never be fulfilled in a pure sense by worldly sources.

➤ Using the Process Way of Life leads to a state of internal balance.

➤ The understanding that balancing your physical, intellectual, emotional, and spiritual attributes creates pure love.

➤ The movement away from the worldly notion of love to one that is defined as a pure energy source, and a natural byproduct of internal balance.

Love does not exist outside of you. As with all of your processes, it lives inside of you. If you are willing to commit yourself to the time and effort it takes to make the Process Way of Life work for you, you will move to a state of internal balance, and you will love yourself. When this happens, you will understand what love is, and how to express it. Then you can extend it outward to others.

 ## TIME TO TAKE ACTION

1. With a renewed understanding of what love can be, it's important to renew your commitment to the Process Way of Life. If you want pure love, stay committed to your processes. Look at yourself in the mirror. Meet your eyes and affirm your commitment. Affirm it regularly.

2. Abandon the traditional concept of love. Love lives on the inside, and is born of internal balance.

3. Understand that love, like all our processes, is alive in you. Since it is alive, the potential for continued growth, and the ability to continue to stimulate your growth, your peace of mind, and your fulfillment, are enhanced. Thus, it is imperative that you continue to provide your processes with the fuel for the growth you are seeking.

4. Remember that the Process Way of Life is just that: a way of life. Pure love is the result of your processes leading to internal balance. Work with your processes every day. Apply them to everyone and everything that you encounter. Every day, plan what you are scheduling, and how you are going to incorporate your processes into it. Each evening, review your day, and how you used your processes. Repeat this every day.

5. Enjoy the Process Way of Life and the journey it can provide. Love your new life enough to commit yourself to it. Make it part of everything you do.

 ## DRIVING IT HOME

The ability to love has been inside of you from the moment you were born. You were born with the capacity for internal balance. By focusing on your process of internal growth, you begin to reverse worldly pressures, and restore the internal balance which is the pathway to pure love. Then, you will begin to see the development of an energy source that is pure and good. When this happens, you will understand what love is, and you will love yourself into the person you are becoming.

**YOUR DECLARATION IS**: *I will stay close to my processes;*
*I will love!*

 ## ONWARD

Pure love generated from internal balance lives inside you. It lives inside all of us. The Process Way of Life culminates as you turn this pure love outward and embrace your world, as I will show you in the next chapter.

◇◇◇◇◇◇◇◇◇◇◇◇◇

# CHAPTER 34

# Extending Pure Love to Others

## INTERNAL BALANCE, AND THE NEW LOVING YOU

*Move the balanced person you've become outward, and let yourself love others. Then, you can become someone who can love your whole world, and be loved.*

---

**PROCESSES TO EMPLOY:** Brutal Honesty, I Over E, Present/ Understand/Fix, Slowing Down Life's Pace, Commitment, Dignity, Fact-Finding, Faith, Gratitude, Honor, Humility, In Service, Internal Balance, Internal Focus, Pure Love, Trust, Wisdom

---

ONE OF THE PRIMARY OBJECTIVES of the Process Way of Life is to become a loving person who can love yourself and others, and be loved by them. Learning to love yourself and to apply love to others in your life is another defining measure of the Process Way of Life.

### Your Balance, Your Love, Your Way

Before we proceed, it's important to understand that internal balance is not a collective destination. By this, I mean that not everyone's internal balance looks the same. Let's say we're using a scale from one to ten, with one being the lowest measure, and ten being the highest. When you began your Process Way of Life, you were barely a one or two on the scale. Becoming internally balanced doesn't mean you must ascend to the value of ten. It only means that your physical, intellectual, emotional, and spiritual attributes are in balance. I have been preaching journey living over destination living. If there was some advanced-balance arrival point in the program, it would be a destination. You don't want your growth to rest on the premise that an arrival point exists, and should be the goal of your program.

The goal is not to arrive at a high level. This can happen, but it's not essential to the program. The only goal is to have your four attributes operating in balance. So, it doesn't matter if your point on the scale is a three, a five, or a nine. Loving yourself and beginning to turn that love outward is possible at any personal level of balance. It's your life journey, so it's your own personal balance that is perfect for you. You'll know it's right for you because you will feel the balance, and the love for yourself and others will follow.

## The Real Love Story

Chapter 33 introduced the notion that being balanced internally creates a power source that allows us to experience a loving state of existence. This creates an atmosphere of peace inside us, which is the precursor for the reciprocal nature of love to begin. So, let's explore the practical application of a loving relationship. I've discussed how humans are social beings, and our advanced intellectual and emotional capabilities pave the way for the desire to be attached to other humans. When you love completely, you love physically, intellectually, emotionally, and spiritually. To start extending love outward, these three related factors must be understood:

1. Love is a state of internal balance that produces a pure, living energy source.

2. This pure, living energy allows you to create a loving give-and-take relationship with another person in a loving environment.

3. A loving environment is the outward expression of your internal balance. It creates a tender, trusting, and warm place for pure love to be expressed.

As internal balance is developing inside you, you develop the ability to love yourself. Loving yourself sets the stage for your potential to love another human being. Loving another human being is a three-step process.

➤ First, you must love yourself. As I've already noted, balancing your four attributes presents you with the internal capacity to love yourself.

➤ The second step in the process is turning that love outward. Now, armed with a balanced internal format that reduces the need to be completed by another person, you can simply extend your internal balance (your love) outward to others.

➤ The third step is allowing someone else to love you.

Here's an illustration:

## INSIDE OUT—LOVING ANOTHER, AND SPREADING YOUR LOVE

Eddie and Tina are on a first date. Tina is a confident yet thoughtful person. She is a fourth-grade teacher, enjoys working with animals, and has a part-time job at a local kennel. Eddie is the youngest of three boys, and graduated college with a degree in accounting. Eddie also likes animals, and he, too, works part-time at the kennel, where he met Tina.

Tina has dedicated herself to the Process Way of Life, and is enjoying her first date with Eddie. Understanding internal balance, she is looking for absolutely nothing from Eddie except an enjoyable evening. She is happy with herself, and doesn't need another person to complete her. Tina is not a destination person, so she can enjoy the moment she is living in. She's taking things slowly, without expectations. She feels that peace throughout the evening.

Eddie is a bit more anxious. He thinks he likes Tina already, and is wondering what he would have to do to ensure that she will like him. He's doing the usual things people do on first dates, like trying to impress her just a bit, and being on his best behavior.

As you can see, Tina is already setting the stage for a good experience. Whether or not she and Eddie develop a deeper connection is irrelevant; she's happy with herself, and can be accepting of whatever develops as the evening progresses. Eddie is looking for reassurance, and is not so sure about himself. Now, his emotions are overriding his intellect. Eddie is in a state of imbalance. As a result, he will experience some of the unrest that happens when someone is unsure about something that is important to them. Expect him to be anxious, go too fast, and have his focus on what will happen in the future. It will be difficult for him to enjoy his "in the moment" experience in his current state of imbalance.

Love, in worldly terms, demands internal imbalance so your emotions can be nurtured. Then, you can feel needed and united with the other person, but all of it by means of internal imbalance. It's emotions over everything else. Imagine, you are using the attribute that causes the most chaos to make you feel good. There goes that poor, exhausted little horse pushing that insane emotional cart again.

What would happen if Tina and Eddie were both enjoying their own internal balance? That would mean that each individual would be enjoying the evening in a balanced internal state, and none of their attributes would be overriding the others. Both would be completely relaxed, without requiring anything from the other.

One of the telltale signs of a good balanced relationship is the removal of the anxiety, that heightened neurological state, that makes you think you're in love. The anxiety that comes from initial love, again, is nothing more than your emotions overriding your intellect. If a relationship is, in fact, something that possesses the potential for a peaceful and loving form of fulfillment for each party, this ridiculous emotional dance should never occur.

Our example of Eddie and Tina's first date is a simple illustration regarding how you can use the Process Way of Life and its processes to both love yourself, and to extend your love outward. It, however, isn't only limited to a relationship with another person. Our example simply sets the stage for how you can move internal balance outside of yourself. At this stage in the program, you want to love yourself, love others, and be loved by others. In the bigger picture, however, it's all about becoming a loving person. Remember, learning to trust the processes helped you learn to trust yourself. So trust yourself now. Trust that your internal balance will pave the way for the friendships and relationships that can be so important as your life continues. Use the example as the way you can extend your balanced love outside of yourself to everyone you touch.

## Internal Balance to the Rescue

How many times have you entered what you thought would have been a nice relationship with someone, where you were so excited that you can't wait to see them, only to have that excitement last for a few months, and then slowly, or maybe suddenly disappear? You don't create the balanced internal way of doing things so that you can throw it out of balance to find yourself in what you think is love. That's ludicrous, and contrary to everything that you're doing.

If the relationship is going to last, it progresses calmly, with all internal attributes remaining in balance. This applies to both a romantic relationship, and to all your relationships with others. That's what the Process Way of Life teaches, and that's the format you want to stay committed to. When you move yourself into a new part of your life, and that includes all of your external relationships, you simply refer them back to your processes. Everything will be taken care of there. You will experience an exuberance that you will have never experienced before.

After you begin to love yourself, you don't rush out and attempt to love the rest of the world. You simply want to extend your balanced life journey outward. You're already working with it internally. Now you're going to infuse everything in your external world, including the potential for new friendships and relationships, with the balance you have worked to attain. Internally balanced love, just like internal passion, lives inside you, and moves outward embracing everything it touches.

You're not trying to love another person. You're not trying to assess what their needs are, and then do your best to fulfill them. You are simply applying every part of your balanced format, and that includes all the processes that changed your life, to another person. Remember, the Process Way of Life is a format that can address all the situations in your life. Why would you think it wouldn't work as you extend your love outward? Oh, and relax. When it comes to your romance, there will be plenty of excitement. You're not sacrificing that; you're just side-stepping the insanity, and the eventual maniacal fallout.

Allowing others to love you is simply a matter of allowing them to share their balanced internal processes with you. So, looking back to Tina and Eddie; while Tina is infusing her date with her balanced format, she is also allowing Eddie to bring his, should it exist, to her. Now, if Eddie is also working to balance himself internally, Tina will know this quickly. She will feel the peace he is displaying. If, on the other hand, as we saw in the example, if Eddie was not working with a balanced internal format, Tina will know this. Tina will then use that information to decide whether or not she wants to see Eddie again. This is how you need to address *all of your relationships*. Use your processes, and stay focused on what I have discussed to bring the loving potential of the Process Way of Life to everyone in your world.

Creating a loving relationship, and in the end, a loving life with a balanced internal format, is really a very simple process. The processes you are working with create internal balance, which is alive in you, and allows you to love both the balance, and yourself. When you love yourself, you may use the same processes which are creating internal balance for you, and express those in situations which may potentially evolve into loving friendships, and personal relationships.

In those situations, you can keep yourself open and allow others to express themselves, and their love, to you. Refer your new relationships to your processes, and allow them to work their magic. Love yourself, love others, and be loved by them—pure and perfect.

 ## TIME TO TAKE ACTION

1. When it comes to developing new relationships with others, have no expectations or goals aside from enjoying time with them. Use your processes. Stay in the moment, go slow, assess the situation, and gather the facts, as I presented in Chapters 2, 3, 4, and 5.

2. Remember, you don't need this new relationship. You already have all you need. Proceed forward with the notion of simply appreciating a new friend or relationship partner.

3. Assess whether or not the other person is also working to balance themselves internally. If they are, there is a compatibility factor, and this compatibility factor is a simply wonderful way to start your new relationship. Everything else develops from there.

4. No potential love interest becomes more important than your processes. The attempt to love anyone in your life always follows the direction and wisdom that can come from using your processes to make it happen. Stay focused, and never, ever remove that focus from your program.

5. Keep the excitement level down. Enjoy the moment in balance. Balance keeps everything focused, and has an added component of longevity. Learn to appreciate yourself, and another person in any given situation. This is what loving relationships are all about. Relax and enjoy the moment. Let things develop from there.

## DRIVING IT HOME

There is inner peace, and a marvelous energy source that you will receive from a balanced internal way of doing things. This allows you to extend that balance outward, and experience those wonderful feelings in another human being. It lets you know that you can be passionate and fulfilled, without being psychotic. Remember, if you are balanced internally, you will love yourself, and that must come before external relationships. Internal balance sets the stage for all the love you will need, and the exciting potential to extend your loving balance outward.

**YOUR DECLARATION IS**: *I will love myself; I will love my world.*

## ONWARD

The Process Way of Life has provided you with an invaluable new way to live your life. It's time to reflect on how much work you've done, how much you are doing, and how far you have come since you opened this book to page 1.

◇◇◇◇◇◇◇◇◇◇◇◇

# CHAPTER 35

# The Journey Within, and the New You

*You are beautiful! You are great! You are limitless. Trust the spirit inside you, and always believe in yourself!*

---

**PROCESSES TO EMPLOY:** Brutal Honesty, I Over E, Present/ Understand/Fix, Slowing Down Life's Pace, Belief, Commitment, Internal Balance, Pure Love, Trust

---

BEFORE YOU BEGAN THE PROCESS WAY OF LIFE, it's likely that much of the information you received about who you are, and what you are capable of, came from outside sources. You've seen firsthand how fragile a system like this is, and how often it fluctuates. Relying on information coming from outside of you created conflict and confusion, and you realized that you were in pain. You needed to move in different directions.

Your choice to reappraise, and subsequently to reconstruct the conditions of your life and take it off autopilot, motivated you to remove toxic situations and people who were polluting the way you were thinking. This was the first step in the growth you needed to begin the repair process that has led you to the happiness and fulfillment you are realizing today. Following a much-needed purging of the negativity you brought in from outside of yourself, and from your own internal antagonizers, you began to incorporate an array of new processes that became the foundation for the change you so desperately needed.

## You Accepted the Challenge

You now understand that all life is a process. Everything you do is dependent upon the processes you choose to nurture and grow within you. You created a new awareness, not only of how accountable you must be to yourself, but how much potential lies within you. By taking control of your own life and accepting the responsibility for your own decisions, you laid the framework for the process-driven growth that would follow.

Those processes became the underpinning for everything you would do to remove yourself from negativity. They became the positive and fulfilling infrastructure you needed to stabilize what was previously a conflicted and confused way of thinking. You now know you must keep life's pace slow, and stay in tune with its natural flow. You are brutally honest with yourself, and you consciously put your intellect before our emotions. The facts are the facts, and they never change. You embraced that. You stopped letting fear run your life, and you saw how envy was stealing so much of your energy. You live in today, and in the moment.

Quick fixes became a thing of the past, and you accepted the challenge of investing the time it takes for growth to become reality. You saw how useless anger is, and how it can be transformed into positive energy. You began taking care of your body, and you know that decisions need to be made with information that sees the big picture.

You understand that the little steps and the little gains in life are the most important. You're setting goals instead of destinations, and you realize how important the journey is, with all its marvelous daily gifts. Every day of your life and every minute of your life is precious, and must never be wasted. You also understand how important balance is among your physical, intellectual, emotional, and spiritual attributes.

You feel the processes alive inside you, and leading you to a balanced state of living that is also alive, producing an energy source that is pure and loving. You have become a humble and grateful person who is willing to share your gifts with others unconditionally. The journey within has truly been remarkable.

## The Pure, Simple, Wonderful, Loving Journey: You!

As you progress, you must realize that you will continue to be challenged. You can accept those challenges because you learned to trust your Process Way of Life, and now you trust yourself. Your processes have been with you all along, and they will never let you down. You know you can apply them in your life, regardless of what you are faced with. The change from destination to journey-oriented people has an unmatched magnificence all its own. Life is truly a gift. You understand that now. You don't need the splendor of the all-inspiring destinations to convince you that you are alive. Every breath you take is a living miracle. You know that, too.

The most important gift you received was the process that helped you understand that you are a good person who can love yourself and others. You are a gift to yourself and to the world. You are our own perfect hero. Your abilities and your potentialities have become limitless.

The trust you have in yourself and in the processes which have changed your life and will continue to guide you through the rest of your days, is something to be cherished. Life was meant to be lived simply, all the time. You never understood that. You understand that internal balance has removed superficial and unnecessary desires from your life, and that you are complete.

## You Were Always Beautiful; Believe in Yourself, Forever! BE!

You began as a person with questionable identity, redefined yourself, came to like yourself, and in the end, understand how to love yourself, and the rest of the world. You learned that morality, honor, and dignity are more important than your worldly desires.

As you progressed in the Process Way of Life, you began to understand what faith is, and how advantageous it is to have it in your process toolbox. As the Process Way of Life continued to evolve, something else has begun to happen. The faith in and love of the processes, which are alive inside of you, has led to a wonderful sense of belief in your own capabilities, and the perfect person you were created to be.

Finally, you began to believe in yourself. This happened because the processes, which began as routine chores, have evolved into not only what you are doing, but who you are. As you trust the processes, love the processes, and believe in the processes, you can't help but attach those same feelings to yourself. You are now a believer in yourself. It's an absolutely wonderful place to be.

## ⏱ TIME TO TAKE ACTION WITH A BIG PAT ON THE BACK

1. Trust your processes, and know that they have always been there for you, and they always will.

2. Be honest. Make the truth your best friend.

3. Live life to the fullest in each and every second that is available to you. Waste nothing, and appreciate everything.

4. Enjoy your life, and laugh as much as you can.

5. Look at everything around you, and understand all the gifts you have.

6. Take nothing for granted, and appreciate everything that comes into your life. Be grateful for every moment that is your life.

7. Touch everything and everyone, and don't be afraid to let others touch you.

8. Think good thoughts as much as you possibly can. Fortify the world inside you with positive energy.

9. Embrace yourself and embrace your world. The whole world is there for you. Pull it in close, and trust that through your processes and your balance, it will not hurt you.

10. Forgive yourself and others. This helps you keep your energy positive.

11. Wonderful gifts have been given to you. Share them freely, and love everyone you share them with. Always be in service of others.

12. Be passionate from the inside, and attach that passion to everyone and everything in your world.

13. Stay in today. Let go of all that is past, and disconnect yourself from the anxiety of the future.

14. Love for free. Expect nothing in return.

15. Trust that your processes will always be there for you. They always have been. Through them, you will trust yourself.

16. Have faith, and be willing to define and embrace something bigger than yourself.

17. Take risks. Stretch beyond your own perceived limits.

18. Love the journey that is your life. Don't worry about quick fixes and glorious destinations. Love every minute of your marvelous life journey.

19. Remember internal balance. We are intellectual, emotional, physical, and spiritual beings. Allow your processes to keep you in a balanced internal state. When you are there, pure love is possible, and happiness and fulfillment are yours.

20. Enjoy everyone and every part of your wonderful life. You took the time to fix it.

##  DRIVING IT HOME

Everything you need to live a balanced and loving life is now in place. The key remains in your hands. Don't follow the trendsetters: be the trend! Don't ride someone else's wave: be the wave! Don't try to be someone else: be yourself! Keep using your processes; never abandon them, and bring everyone and everything you experience back to the new loving energy source that guides your life. You are the author of your own beautiful journey forward. Love the person you are because you took the time to make yourself who you are. **BE!**

**YOUR DECLARATION IS:** *I will stay beautiful; I will stay great; I will believe! I will love! I will BE!*

##  ONWARD

You have made many important changes in your life by dedicating time and effort to the Process Way of Life. To be sure that they are lasting changes, the next chapter provides you with one last process: the gift of housekeeping.

◇◇◇◇◇◇◇◇◇◇◇◇

# CHAPTER 36

# Good Housekeeping

## THE NEVER-ENDING PROCESS GIFT

*Regardless of how far you come in life, every so often, a good housecleaning is in order.*

---

**PROCESSES TO EMPLOY:** Brutal Honesty, I Over E, Present/ Understand/Fix, Slowing Down Life's Pace, Boundary-Setting, Eliminating Toxic People, Housekeeping, Intelligent Decision- Making, Life Inventory, System Maintenance

---

THROUGH THE PROCESS WAY OF LIFE, you have moved your life from a place of imbalance to one of internal balance. The logical conclusion is that once you have achieved balance, your life will remain this way, and old problems will no longer cause you difficulty. That's not exactly how it goes, though.

Your life will not remain in balance without your continued attention, because people and events can throw you out of sync from time to time. When this happens, you will need to make a conscious effort to right your process-ship, and restore your internal balance. Housekeeping makes that happen.

Toxic people aren't so good at obeying your newfound boundaries. These undesirable guests repeatedly show up at your doorstep, uninvited and unwelcome. Sometimes they'll come from right inside your own mind. Logic would have you assuming that if you eliminated the toxic effects of these people and past events, you shouldn't have to re-involve yourself with these misery-laden vagabonds. If this is what you're thinking, well, think again. You see, those vagabonds have other ideas, and it's important that you be willing to "houseclean" them from your world every so often. Let's illustrate:

## DRIP, DROP

Five years ago, you had the local roofing company at your home to repair your leaky roof. They guaranteed that the roof would protect your home for twenty years. In fact, they gave you a written warranty to back up their claim. Now, here you are just a quarter of the way through that legal and binding pledge, and little droplets of water are sneaking through the ceiling in your dining room, working their way down your new chandelier, and onto your shiny dining-room table. You are fit to be tied. Those miserable so-and-sos guaranteed the job, and the problem is back, worse than it was before. How could this happen? You did everything you were supposed to do to fix the problem, and they promised that it would work.

Just because you did the work to make yourself healthier, wiser, and stronger doesn't necessarily mean that people and issues, both internal and external, won't find their way back into your life. Life doesn't stop just because you made some improvements. Life is an ongoing affair, and the challenges inherent in living in an unstable world will continuously reappear. It's so important to understand this. This life is fluid and ongoing, and it is absolutely loaded with wonderful people and events, while at the same time being infested with those little toxins and demons you would like to strangle, especially on their return visits.

You didn't make changes in yourself with the assumption that the rest of the world would enthusiastically cooperate with your Process Way of Life. In fact, have no expectation whatsoever that the outside world is going to see it your way. That was never part of the plan. If things could work that way, why spend so much time changing yourself? You are changing who you are from the inside so that you can be ready now, and at any time in the future, for the cards that life deals you. When you become strong on the inside, you can be better equipped to keep negative and toxic intruders from infiltrating your life, and bringing your process-house down again.

## The Never-Ending Story

Housekeeping is an ongoing state of affairs. It's the process checks and balances that never stops. Know that if you remain committed to your processes with the understanding that all happy people adjust, transition, and defend their gains on a routine basis, the external world becomes that much less oppressive. It's about staying close to your processes, and applying and reapplying them routinely. Housekeeping is one of them. When you stay close to the processes, all return visitors are assigned to the new stronger version of you, and the negative and toxic invaders will perish there. Follow these steps, and keep your process life-house strong:

## The 7 Steps for Successful Housecleaning

1. Be ready for return visitors; they're coming.

2. Identify your new intruder.

3. Be honest about what you are seeing.

4. Slow down, and keep your emotions in check.

5. Gather all the necessary facts.

6. Based on the facts, develop a plan to address the problem.

7. Execute your plan completely; use your processes.

Housekeeping simply tells you to remain on guard for the little invasions from these unwanted visitors, so you may remove them from your world before they can have a negative impact on you. It's a wonderful forward process ally.

If you keep focusing on you, and staying committed to the

Process Way of Life, repeated housekeeping does nothing more than show you just how strong are. You've become a process-armed, internally-charged, balanced, independent, loving warrior. You're getting stronger every day. Love yourself, and the wonderful world you are creating. Live happy, and be ready to protect your wonderful new world.

##  TIME TO TAKE ACTION FOR ONE LAST TIME

1. Address the return visitor with your intellect. There is no room for emotion here. Think, don't react.

2. Remember that this is a return visit. You fixed it the first time, so you know exactly what to do on the return visit. Use the processes that apply to the return visit.

3. Never be surprised by return visitors. Some come from the outside, and some may be your own. Expect that they may return. This will reduce a return visitor's shock value, and your emotional response to it.

4. Accept the challenge with confidence and the understanding that you are capable of addressing it, because you are. Every successful housecleaning attempt increases your confidence.

##  DRIVING IT HOME

Keep cleaning house. While you're doing so, understand how far you've come, how capable you are becoming, and how ready you are for a wonderful life. It's never about how many times you clean your house. It's about how strong you are because you do.

**YOUR DECLARATION IS:** *I made the gains, I'm keeping the gains, I'm loving my world.*

# The Fix Yourself Handbook—
## Conclusion

REMEMBER THAT YOUR PROGRESSION THROUGH the Process Way of Life will always be a work in progress. There is no arrival point. I wrote the book in journey form to help you understand how the Process Way of Life works. Continue reading the book. Continue applying the processes in your life. Finishing the book doesn't mean you finished the program.

Keep reading it, and keep applying the principles in your life. You will feel the changes you are making to become a loving person throughout the program, as they slowly develop in you. Simply stay committed to the Process Way of Life, and when enough time has elapsed, you will be able to identify your internal balance as you feel it, little by little.

The Process Way of Life was never meant to be a quick fix, and you were never meant to realize the wonderful gains you are making in your life right away. It's an every day, in the moment program that helps you love yourself, and the rest of your world. Just focus on that. Be that journey person, and love the beautiful world you are creating inside yourself, and for the rest of your world.

Stay committed to the Process Way of Life. Never, ever quit, and your greatness will embrace the world. It's you who took the time to love yourself into the person you are becoming. Everything you ever needed has always been inside you. You know that now. Keep loving yourself into a new and more exciting life journey. As you do, wrap your love around everyone and everything you touch. **Stay beautiful! Stay great! Love!**

# About the Author

**Faust A. Ruggiero's** professional career spans almost forty years, and is diversified and compelling, as it has consistently established new and exciting cutting-edge counseling programs in its pursuit of professional excellence and personal life enhancement. He is a published research author, clinical trainer, and a therapist who has worked in settings that have included clinics for deaf children, prisons, nursing homes, substance abuse centers, inpatient facilities, and as the President of the Community Psychological Center in Bangor, Pennsylvania. In that capacity, he developed the Process Way of Life counseling program, and has developed it into a formal text presented in the *Fix Yourself Handbook.*

Upon graduating from Mansfield University in 1977, Mr. Ruggiero enrolled in the graduate program in psychology at Illinois State University. There, with a dual major in clinical and developmental psychology with a minor in research, he assisted in the publication of several research articles, including his thesis "The effects of prosocial and antisocial television programs on the cognitions of children."

Upon leaving graduate school, Mr. Ruggiero began working with Antoinette Goffredo counseling services providing psychological intervention to adolescent deaf children. There, he helped Ms. Goffredo develop a behavioral management program for profoundly deaf children with residual hearing.

In 1982, he accepted a position with the Lehigh Valley Alcohol Counseling Center. There he provided individual counseling services to clientele suffering from alcohol abuse and addiction, including the introduction to both the twelve-step recovery process, and family and intervention services. It was at the alcohol counseling center where Mr. Ruggiero was asked to develop a Phase 2 counseling program for individuals convicted of drunk driving offenses.

In 1984, Mr. Ruggiero left the Alcohol Counseling Center to pursue a treatment position at Northampton County prison. There he provided psychological and substance abuse intake and counseling services to inmates. He coordinated all substance abuse services and program development services for inmates. In 1986, he obtained his certification in substance abuse treatment in the state of Pennsylvania.

He left Northampton County prison in 1989 to pursue his endeavors at the Community Psychological Center on a full-time basis. As president of the Community Psychological Center, Mr. Ruggiero continued to provide services to individuals, families, those suffering with substance abuse, abused women and women in transition, and couples and marriage counseling. In 1994, Mr. Ruggiero accepted an invitation to become a trainer for the Department of Health in Pennsylvania.

Mr. Ruggiero also provides counseling services for first responders, law enforcement, and other emergency personnel. Following several years of experimentation regarding the various therapeutic approaches, Mr. Ruggiero developed and began utilizing the Process Way of Life Program. The program consists of over fifty internal human processes, which can be accessed and developed to help clients address the various conditions which were affecting their lives. After the program was developed, it was rigorously researched and tested, and changes were made culminating in the approach presently being used by Mr. Ruggiero at the Community Psychological Center.

In the summer of 2016, Mr. Ruggiero decided to develop the Process Life Program into a text that can be published, and would help people in need address the difficult situations that are affecting their lives. *The Fix Yourself Handbook* was completed in 2019.

Visit www.faustruggiero.com